NEW YORK
in Stride

First published in the United States of America in 2020
by Rizzoli International Publications, Inc.
300 Park Avenue South
New York, NY 10010
www.rizzoliusa.com

Publisher: Charles Miers
Editorial Direction: Martynka Wawrzyniak
Design: Claudia Wu
Production Manager: Colin Hough Trapp
Managing Editor: Lynn Scrabis

2020 2021 2022 2023/ 10 9 8 7 6 5 4 3 2 1

Distributed in the U.S. trade by Random House, New York
Printed in China
ISBN: 978-0-8478-6660-1
Library of Congress Control Number: 2019945679

Visit us online:
Facebook.com/RizzoliNewYork | Twitter: @Rizzoli_Books | Instagram.com/RizzoliBooks
Pinterest.com/RizzoliBooks | Youtube.com/user/RizzoliNY | Issuu.com/Rizzoli

NEW YORK
in Stride

AN INSIDER'S WALKING GUIDE

by Jessie Kanelos Weiner & Jacob Lehman

New York · Paris · London · Milan

CONTENTS

HUDSON RIVER

BLEECKER ST

ONE WAY

NO STOPPING
ANYTIME

EAST RIVER

ROOSEVELT ISLAND

EAST RIVER FERRY

LOVE

INTRODUCTION

Of all the cities in the world, New York is the one people think they know best when they haven't been here at all. We know the West Village from Bob Dylan album covers and Hitchcock films, Brooklyn Heights from Truman Capote, and Harlem from Langston Hughes. We know the architecture from Berenice Abbott's photographs, the subway from Bruce Davidson's, and the faces of the city from Humans of New York. We know what lunch is like at Katz's with Harry and Sally, and what dinner at the Carnegie Deli is like with Broadway Danny Rose. And we know what the Empire State Building looks like when we start playing with Legos.

So deeply imprinted in global culture is this iconic vision of the city that "I Love NY" is a refrain and a fashion accessory, even for those who've never set foot in the city. It's easy for visitors to focus their time here on making their way to the many landmarks that have contributed to New York's reputation. But rather than gear another guide book around just those sights and attractions themselves, we want instead to give readers a glimpse of how locals make the most of the city—where the journey can be as important as the destination, and where a casual stroll to pick up a coffee might lead you past treasured secrets and beloved monuments in equal measure.

One thing not everybody knows about New York is that it's a walking city: more than any other city in America, it's a place best explored, most fully enjoyed, and only truly learned on foot. Wherever you go there are windows to look in, stoops to sit on, shops to visit, artworks to look at, people to bump into, or cafés to watch them from. Whether you're in the thick of midtown Manhattan or a residential part of Brooklyn, the characters of the city's districts can change from one block to the next. And with an ever-increasing network of bicycle lanes and ferry routes, it's now easier than ever to get around at street level: with judicious use of Citi Bikes and water taxis, New Yorkers can broaden their walks around neighborhoods and even between boroughs without suffering in traffic or relying too heavily on the subway.

And so, inspired by Jessie's book, *Paris in Stride,* we outlined walking itineraries that take you through some of the city's most interesting and varied neighborhoods, just as locals might explore them. Each walk opens with a map detailing the suggested route and is followed by descriptions and beautiful illustrations of some of the sights and attractions you'll encounter along the way, from historic buildings and unexpected views to wonderful shops and restaurants. And dotted among the walks are sections focusing on aspects of the city that make New York unique—public artworks hiding in plain sight, lesser-known museums, parks off the beaten track—as well as guides to understanding fundamentals of city life from getting around to finding the best of its beloved street food.

After more than fifteen years as a New Yorker, and with Murray, my faithful corgi, walking by my side, I've covered a lot of ground and learned plenty of the city's secrets. Knowing the most relaxing way to navigate the busy streets of SoHo, or where to go for a really good bagel, or the best way to explore the Red Hook waterfront—or where to find the best dog runs—is something that can only

come through those years of curiosity and experience. With *New York in Stride* tucked in your bag or your pocket, we hope to share that experience with you by suggesting these walks as ways to begin your exploration of the city; and invite you to bring your own curiosity and sense of adventure to inspire you from there.

—*Jacob and Jessie*

GETTING AROUND

New York is a city made for walking—but it's also a big place, where people rely on myriad transport options to get around. Along with the mass transit system, there are a handful of options it's worth learning about—even if just to get you to the starting point of a walk or to take you home after one.

SUBWAY

The Metrocard is any New Yorker's (and every visitor's) most valuable tool. The subway system in New York is vast and can be difficult to grasp at first, but covers the entire city twenty-four hours a day, from the parks at the top of the Bronx to the beaches at the
bottom of Brooklyn. To keep up with other cosmopolitan counterparts, the subway is improving all the time, with a helpful app for smartphones and arrivals monitors and touchscreen information booths at many stations. Just make sure you swipe your card quickly enough at the gate; get out of the way when people want to get off; and don't trust the single empty car in an otherwise crowded train...

BUSES

The Metrocard works on the city's buses, too. Thanks to the city's grid system, bus routes in New York are relatively easy to use: they tend to go generally uptown, downtown, or across town. While typically slower than the subway, they often reach blocks the subway doesn't, and can be particularly helpful on crosstown Manhattan adventures, where the subway lines run mostly up- and downtown.

CABS

Even with the rise of apps like Uber and Lyft, iconic New York City yellow taxis still rule the streets. While the reality is both less gritty than

De Niro's *Taxi Driver* and less romantic than a cabbie appearing magically to a doorman's whistle, riding in taxis is comfortable and comparatively affordable, and finding one in the busier parts of town is usually easy. Just beware the witching hour, between 4 p.m. and 5 p.m., when drivers change shifts and are less inclined to pick up fares going anywhere that's not in the direction of their home garage.

FERRIES

New York is a coastal city surrounded by water—so it makes sense that New Yorkers use the waterways to travel. There are a number of nautical options for getting around, from the Staten Island Ferry (which is free) to water taxis that can take you to Governor's Island, Red Hook, Rockaway Beach, and beyond. The East River Ferry is particularly useful and is the most commonly used by commuters; its route runs from Wall Street below the South Street Seaport all the way up the Brooklyn waterfront to Long Island City in Queens and across to East 34th Street in Midtown Manhattan.

CITI BIKE

Inspired by bike-sharing programs in European capital cities, Citi Bikes are a hugely popular way to get around for locals and tourists alike. With more than 750 stations dotted around the city (and a helpful app to locate them), it's a great way to make quick and pleasant

trips—and to see the sights as you go instead of traveling underground. New York's bicycle paths have grown in number and improved in quality in recent years, so cycling around the city is safer than it's ever been.

UPTOWN

UPTOWN TRAINS

Nothing says "classic New York" like Uptown Manhattan. More than the ever-changing neighborhoods downtown or the evolving boroughs around it, the majesty of its wide avenues and the charm of its tree-lined cross streets still define the city at its most romantic. The mighty residential buildings that line the avenues on either side of the park are embodiments of the area's history and character—from the luxurious austerity of the east side to the bohemian grandeur of the west. On the Upper East Side are Gracie Mansion, Museum Mile, high-end stores, and Jackie O'Nassis's church; on the Upper West Side are the Historical Society, the Beacon Theatre, chocolate chip cookies, and John Lennon's towers. And in between, stroll across Central Park, whose meadows give the greatest views of the iconic uptown skylines. A walk from the Upper East Side across the park to the Upper West Side is not only a walk through the most beautiful architecture in the city, nor just a tour of its most significant cultural landmarks—it's also a reminder of how extraordinary it is that so much is contained on an island narrow enough to cross in an afternoon.

❶ GRACIE MANSION

At the very eastern edge of Manhattan, surveying the "Hell's Gate" channel of the East River, Roosevelt Island, Randall's Island, and Queens and the Bronx beyond, stands the city's oldest official residence. Built in 1799 by shipping magnate Archibald Gracie, the house was a private residence for almost a century, until the city converted it to municipal property as a part of its surrounding Carl Schurz Park in 1896. The official residence of the incumbent city mayors since 1942, the mansion has been home to some of the most remarkable figures in New York's recent history, from Fiorello LaGuardia to Rudy Giuliani. With its Federal-style architecture, the house itself cuts a quaint and anachronistic figure against the backdrop of the surrounding neighborhoods. Make an appointment to tour the house or just explore Carl Schurz Park and take in the views at the waterfront—and imagine yourself mayor for the day. ***East 88th Street at East End Avenue, New York, NY 10028***

❷ CHURCH OF ST. THOMAS MORE

The second oldest church on the Upper East Side has one of the most interesting histories. Built in the late nineteenth century, the Church of St. Thomas More was modeled by anglophile architects of the Church of St. Martin's in Gospel Oak, in London—like the Cloisters, it's a replica of something older and European in the heart of Manhattan. Though it's been dwarfed in the last century by taller buildings around it, the church retains an almost village-like charm, with a stunning stained-glass window inside and a small garden around the exterior. It was famously the church of Jacqueline Kennedy Onassis, who held a Mass here for JFK every year after his assassination. *65 East 89th Street, New York, NY 10128*

❸ CORNER BOOKSTORE

The only independent bookshop in this area of the Upper East Side, known as Carnegie Hill, the Corner Bookstore has been a local's favorite since it opened more than forty years ago. Its beautiful windows are always filled with changing displays of bestsellers, and the facade—often with flowers overhanging the sign above—hasn't

changed since 1978. A sign of a good shop is when its staff stick around, and some of the passionate and highly literary booksellers at the Corner Bookstore have been stocking the shelves here for more than fifteen years. Surprisingly for such a modestly sized store, it's a hub for literary events and readings and has a well-considered selection of adult fiction and nonfiction books. *1313 Madison Avenue, New York, NY 10128*

❹ COOPER HEWITT, SMITHSONIAN DESIGN MUSEUM

This remarkable museum is set within the equally remarkable Carnegie Mansion, which was built between 1899 and 1902 for industrial magnate Andrew Carnegie (for whom this part of the Upper East Side came to be named). The magnificent Georgian-style house was a private residence for the Carnegies until 1946, was purchased by the Smithsonian Institution in 1972, and became the home for the Cooper Hewitt Museum in 1976. The Cooper Hewitt's collections are extraordinary, spanning centuries of design in every field and works in every medium. The museum makes spectacular use of the building, with the installation of engaging graphic or technological exhibitions creating intriguing juxtapositions within the Georgian interiors and with a book and gift store occupying the beautifully preserved conservatory that looks out over the mansion's private gardens. *2 East 91st Street, New York, NY 10128*

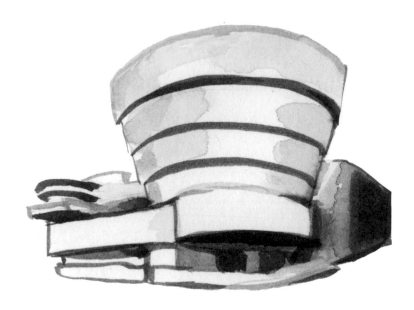

⑤ SOLOMON R. GUGGENHEIM MUSEUM

Probably the most iconic museum building in the world, the Guggenheim was designed by the American architect Frank Lloyd Wright and completed in 1959 (with a neighboring building added in 1992). The famous spiral invites visitors to see works of art in a unique way, unlike any other museum or gallery space in the world, by ascending and descending the gently curving walkway and discovering adjoining rooms along the way. The colossal open space in the center of the spiral allows large-scale installations to be hung dramatically over the lobby. The Guggenheim Foundation's collection focuses on Impressionist, Postimpressionist, and Modern art and includes works from the most significant names in recent centuries, from Marc

Chagall and Vassily Kandinksy to Paul Klee and Piet Mondrian. No matter what's on display, the experience of the architecture alone is worth a visit. *1071 Fifth Avenue, New York, NY 10128*

❻ NEUE GALERIE

Dedicated to Austrian and German art of the late nineteenth and early twentieth centuries, Neue Galerie is the city's most elegant museum. All the works in the museum's collection—from its Bauhaus pieces to its archive of masterpieces by Gustav Klimt and Egon Schiele to its Wiener Werkstätte objects—are owned by the museum itself, the estate of the collector and art dealer Serge Sabarsky, or the philanthropist Ronald S. Lauder. Set within the stunning Beaux-Arts William Starr Miller House, the museum also houses one of the most beautiful restaurants in the city—Café Sabarsky, on the ground floor, whose wood-paneled windows look out onto Fifth Avenue and Central Park, and whose menu (under the celebrated Austrian restaurateur Kurt Gutenbrunner) serves classic Viennese coffees and German pastries in keeping with the atmosphere of the collections. *1048 Fifth Avenue, New York, NY 10028*

❼ THE METROPOLITAN MUSEUM OF ART

No exploration of Museum Mile would be complete without a visit to the Met, the largest museum in the country and one of the most-visited art institutions in the world. To take in the museum's vast collections would warrant a full day of walking on its own—but for those out for a walk across the city, one often overlooked part of the museum is worth finding in particular: the roof. The Iris and

B. Gerald Cantor rooftop garden, situated on the western side of the museum, affords the most spectacular view of Central Park and the surrounding skyline and is often decorated with large-scale installations from artists whose work is exhibited within the museum. **1000 Fifth Avenue, New York, NY 10028**

❽ THE 79ᵀᴴ STREET TRANSVERSE

To cross Central Park without getting lost is a skill it takes New Yorkers years to learn. But if you enter the park next to the Met, just north of the 79th Street Transverse—the road in the center of the park that allows traffic through—you'll be guided by the pathways on a scenic walk that takes you by some of the park's best-known features, from Turtle Pond to the Delacorte Theater, and leads you to the 81st Street exit immediately opposite the American Museum of Natural History. **East 79th Street to West 81st Street, Central Park, New York, NY**

❾ THE AMERICAN MUSEUM OF NATURAL HISTORY

One of the largest and most beautiful museums in the world, the American Museum of Natural History takes hold of any imagination, no matter what age. Housed in a complex of grand buildings, different parts dating from the late nineteenth century to the 1930s, the museum is best known for its incredible dioramas of animals in their native landscapes (which feel almost like scenes from a Wes Anderson film) and for its colossal fiberglass model of a blue whale, which hangs majestically over the Milstein Hall of Ocean Life. The distinctive Hayden Planetarium, housed in the Rose Center for Earth and Space, a futuristic building to the north of the main museum, is a sight to behold at night, when it's lit as beautifully as the panoramic light shows displayed within. *Central Park West at West 79th Street, New York, NY 10024*

❿ NEW-YORK HISTORICAL SOCIETY

The New-York Historical Society's museum, first opened in 1804, is the oldest in New York, with collections of artwork and documents chronicling the history of both the city and the country. The building itself is magisterial, with a grand Roman entrance on Central Park West that's rivaled only by the Met across the park. The Patricia D. Klingenstein Library inside is one of the most spectacular rooms in the city, with stained-glass windows filtering in the light from the park and a balcony supported by Neoclassical pillars towering above the reading room. *170 Central Park West, New York, NY 10024*

⑪ SAN REMO BUILDING

Perhaps the most rec-
ognizable silhouette of
Central Park's skyline,
the San Remo Building,
completed in 1931, is
one of New York's most
famous residences and
one of the iconic struc-
tures that defines the
character of the Upper
West Side. Its towers are
visible from anywhere in
the park and have been
home to a glittering list
of the city's most cel-
ebrated residents, from
Stephen Sondheim to
Diane Keaton—but not
to Madonna, who was allegedly rejected by the building's co-op
board when she applied for an apartment here. *Central Park West
between West 74th and West 75th Streets, New York, NY 10024*

⑫ LEVAIN BAKERY

Like Magnolia downtown, Levain is a bakery that is simply never without a line. So
popular are their cookies, hamantaschen,
breads, and pastries that people travel from

far and wide to queue before they open and throughout the day. So bewitching is the aroma of treats baking in ovens from their tiny storefront that the entire block on 74th Street smells of homemade cookies, and passersby find themselves wandering over to join the line without even realizing what they're doing. A perfect snack to carry to Central Park. *167 West 74th Street, New York, NY 10023*

⑬ ANSONIA BUILDING

Another defining facade of the Upper West Side is that of the Ansonia, a colossal Beaux-Arts building originally designed to be a hotel in 1904. Conceived to be the epitome of luxury, the building is equipped with a pneumatic system of tunnels to carry messages between rooms and the staff, and for its first few years of existence housed a small farm on its rooftop. Now one of the most expensive apartment buildings in the city, the Ansonia has been home over the years to many famous New Yorkers, from Babe Ruth to Isaac Bashevis Singer. *2109 Broadway, New York, NY 10023*

⑭ BEACON THEATRE

Opened in 1929, the Beacon is one of the city's great old theaters and has the most stunning auditorium anywhere in New York.

If you're lucky enough to see a show here, you'll find decadent tiers of red velvet and gold rising above the curtained stage and the pillared walls and an ornate ceiling decorated with Neoclassical murals, making anything from a concert to a movie feel like the grandest opera. If you're not seeing a show, settle for the sight of the iconic awning outside. *2124 Broadway, New York, NY 10023*

❶❺ APTHORP BUILDING

The magnificent Apthorp building—commissioned by William Waldorf Astor and built in 1908—is a New York City Landmark with a beautifully maintained Renaissance Revival exterior that includes enormous sculptures representing the four seasons above the entrance. The courtyard within the Apthorp is among the loveliest spaces uptown—small enough to feel private and enclosed by the building's beautiful stone walls, but large enough to be light and airy.

It is decorated with trees, manicured gardens, and benches surrounding a fountain. The building was home to, among many other celebrated residents, Nora Ephron, who famously wrote a love letter to the building in *The New Yorker* in 2006. ***2211 Broadway, New York, NY 10024***

ⓖ ZABAR'S

An Upper West Side institution, Zabar's is about as famous as a supermarket can get; spend any time in the city and you'll see their tote bags everywhere. With an old-fashioned look and feel, the store's many departments cater to all the classic tastes of the archetypal New Yorker, from fresh bagels in the bakery to its legendary smoked fish counter. While it's a true neighborhood market for locals, it's also a place to pick up sandwiches, snacks, or prepared food to go. ***2245 Broadway, New York, NY 10024***

ⓗ BOAT BASIN CAFE

Set within a charming vaulted space above the 79th Street marina, the Boat Basin Cafe is a beautiful reminder of Manhattan's closeness to the water. The Boat Basin itself has been an active marina for almost a century; even Frank Sinatra used to dock his yacht here. Overlooking the river, with tables outside as well as lovely views through the arches from within, it's a wonderful place to end a day watching the sun set over New Jersey. ***West 79th Street at the Hudson River, New York, NY 10024***

MUSEUMS

There's more to New York City's cultural landscape than Museum Mile. Here are just five of the city's "off-Mile" museums that are worth a visit.

LOUIS ARMSTRONG HOUSE MUSEUM

The borough of Queens has a uniquely rich musical history: it's the birthplace of superstars from Paul Simon to Nicki Minaj; the legendary reggae producer Coxsone Dodd ran a record shop here; and a famous mural in the neighborhood of St. Albans memorializes jazz age heroes, from Billie Holiday to Count Basie. The musical jewel in Queens's crown, however, might be the Louis Armstrong House Museum. Beautifully preserved, from his living room to the recording studio built into his study, the museum looks and feels like an architectural portrait of the great man himself. The museum is a short walk from Flushing Meadows park (see page 77).

NEW YORK TRANSIT MUSEUM

The New York City public transit system is one of the oldest and busiest in the world: the subway dates to 1904 and millions of passengers navigate the city on it every day. The Transit Museum in Brooklyn is one of the city's hidden gems, with rotating exhibitions and permanent collections that transform artifacts and records of the MTA's history into surprisingly engaging shows. You can climb aboard a vintage tram car, sit inside a bus driver's cabin, or look at the evolution of the subway through the work of celebrated photographers from Irving Penn to Bruce Davidson. The museum is situated in a former subway station a few blocks from the Brooklyn Historical Society, at the beginning of our Brooklyn Riviera walk (see page 152).

TREASURES IN THE TRASH COLLECTION

Founded and run by one creatively minded sanitation worker, the Treasures in the Trash Collection is an ever-growing assortment of remarkable objects discovered by the city's garbage collectors. With no precisely set criteria, the collection is curated by its founder, Nelson Molina, and includes everything from vintage toy robots to naive paintings and sets of porcelain doorknobs. With such eclectic contents from such humble origins, the museum—with tongue in cheek—presents a fascinating portrait of the city through the "treasures" it throws away. Just a few blocks north of Gracie Mansion at the start of our Uptown Walk (see page 12), the collection is open (selectively) for tours arranged by email.

MMUSEUMM

Founded by Alex Kalman, the son of artist Maira Kalman, and the film directors Josh and Benny Safdie, Mmusuemm is an extraordinary project that redefines the idea of a museum. Unlike the city's larger formal cultural institutions, Mmuseumm occupies a small space behind industrial doors on Cortlandt Alley—a few minutes west of Columbus Park, at the conclusion of our Nolita and Chinatown walk (see page 108). Billing itself as a "modern natural history museum," the tiny pop-up exhibits collections of objects that fall somewhere between evidence of anthropological study and site-specific art installation. The exhibitions are seasonal, running from spring through fall, and travel out of season to related institutions such as the Color Factory in New York or the Skirball in Los Angeles.

CITY RELIQUARY

Behind an unlikely storefront in Williamsburg, several blocks inland from the riverside route of our North Brooklyn walk (see page 140), the City Reliquary is one of the most revealing of New York's museums. A not-for-profit institution, the Reliquary aims to collect and preserve the history of the city through the community itself, sourcing its acquisitions by engaging with New Yorkers young and old and seeking out stories and artifacts from the trivial to the profound. Their rotating exhibitions have touched on topics as diverse in size and scope as an antique boat used to offer pleasure rides around Coney Island to a collection of vintage confetti found beneath the dance floor of the Rainbow Room at Rockefeller Center.

CENTRAL PARK

1. Museum of the City of New York
2. Conservatory Garden
3. Reservoir
4. Arthur Ross Pinetum
5. Hamilton Monument
6. Obelisk
7. Swedish Cottage Marionette Theatre
8. Shakespeare Garden
9. The Ramble
10. Bow Bridge
11. Loeb Boathouse
12. Alice in Wonderland Sculpture
13. Kerbs Boathouse
14. Bethesda Fountain
15. Cherry Hill
16. Le Pain Quotidien
17. The Mall
18. The Carousel
19. Wollman Rink

It's difficult to remember sometimes that Central Park—so utterly iconic of the city's history and image, with its familiar statues, bridges, and skylines—is also simply a local park, a place to jog, walk the dog, or stroll with a morning coffee on the way to the train. Now almost 150 years old, the park of course remains one of the city's top tourist destinations, with crowds drawn every day to its most totemic attractions, from the zoo to the Strawberry Fields memorial to John Lennon.

Situated in the heart of Manhattan, Central Park absorbs and reflects something of the energy of the neighborhoods surrounding it. The south side of the park, bordering midtown and the shopping of Fifth Avenue, is always the busiest, with locals navigating a sea of tourists, caricaturists, and horse-drawn carriages. The northern end of the park, bordering Harlem and farthest from the tourist hub of 59th Street, is the most relaxed, with domino tables and pick-up sports among the monuments and plantings. The Fifth Avenue side, with the formal landscaping of the Conservatory Garden, matches the grandeur of Museum Mile. And Central Park West encapsulates the mix of the historic and the bohemian that defines the Upper West Side. As well as a gentle tour of some of its prettiest areas and lesser-known monuments, a winding route through the whole of the park can reveal not only the variety and beauty of Vaux and Olmsted's landscaping, but the character of the city around it.

❶
MUSEUM OF THE CITY OF NEW YORK

Originally located in Gracie Mansion before it became the official mayoral residence, the Museum of the City of New York was established in 1923 and combines art and history to present and preserve a cultural record of the city. A statue of Alexander Hamilton looks out from the building's facade across Fifth Avenue toward the Vanderbilt Gate, the entrance to Central Park's Conservatory Garden. *1220 Fifth Avenue, New York, NY 10029*

❷ CONSERVATORY GARDEN

The Conservatory Garden is the only formally landscaped garden in Central Park. It's divided into three distinct sections—English, Italian, and French—each with its own features and planting style. The grandest of the three is the Italian garden, with colonnades of crabapple trees facing one another across a manicured lawn and a staircase rising to a pergola draped with climbing wisteria. In the French garden, in reference to the gardens of Versailles, perfect parterres of flowers surround a fountain. But the greatest treasure is the English garden, where wilder flowers and perennials surround the Frances Hodgson Burnett Memorial Fountain, which honors the author of *The Secret Garden*. **Enter at Fifth Avenue and 105th Street or the 106th Street gate inside Central Park**

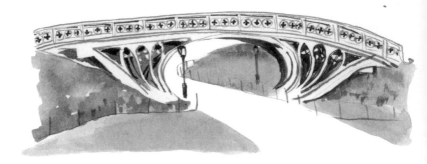

❸ RESERVOIR

The path around the reservoir frames some of the greatest vignettes of the city's skyline, because the space of the water allows for uninterrupted views across the park in any direction. It's a popular place for locals to walk or jog and a lovely route to take when walking south through the park. On the northwestern side of the reservoir, the Gothic Bridge, the loveliest of the three iron bridges that Calvert Vaux designed for the park, crosses the bridle path.

❹ ARTHUR ROSS PINETUM

At the southern end of the reservoir, just below the 86th Street Transverse, the Arthur Ross Pinetum is a small area populated exclusively with evergreens, including species from Japan and the Himalayas. Bordered with rustic wooden fences, the pinetum feels like a different landscape altogether—a park within a park.

❺ HAMILTON MONUMENT

Walk east from the Arthur Ross Pinetum, around the northern end of the Great Lawn and its softball fields, and you'll find the Alexander Hamilton Monument, a grand and heroic statue that was donated to the city by Hamilton's son in 1880.

❻ OBELISK

Directly south of the Hamilton Monument, not far from the Metropolitan Museum of Art, the Obelisk is the oldest sculpture in Central Park. Known as Cleopatra's Needle, it is part of a pair originally made in Egypt around 1450 BC; the other is on the bank of the River Thames in London.

❼ SWEDISH COTTAGE MARIONETTE THEATRE

Walk west across the northern side of Turtle Pond and you'll find the Swedish Cottage Marionette Theatre. An unlikely sight, this wooden alpine cottage was originally built as a model schoolhouse for Sweden's entry in an 1876 exposition; Frederick Law Olmsted bought the building for the park. Since 1947, puppeteers have performed charming productions of children's classics here.

❽ SHAKESPEARE GARDEN

Just to the east of the Swedish Cottage is Central Park's Shakespeare Garden, a beautiful four-acre garden landscaped in an English style and planted with flowers, trees, and herbs referenced (with varying levels of obscurity) in the works of Shakespeare. It's one of the park's more secluded and fragrant spots, as well as a lovely place to sit.

➒ THE RAMBLE

Walk east from the Shakespeare Garden to the Belvedere Castle and south across the 79th Street Transverse and you will find yourself in the Ramble. Designed to be the park's wildest area, the Ramble is a large wood with winding paths, gentle hills, and flights of steps carved into the natural stone outcrops. There are benches and clearings here and there throughout the Ramble, each a beautiful vantage point from which you can take in the remarkable woodland and its wildlife.

➓ BOW BRIDGE

At the southern end of the Ramble, the Bow Bridge leads across the lake to the southern half of the park. Bow Bridge is the most iconic feature of Central Park—the setting for countless movie moments and the picture on countless postcards. It rises gently from the woods of the Ramble and descends in the greenery near Cherry Hill, with its reflection caught perfectly in the still water of the lake below.

⓫ LOEB BOATHOUSE

At the eastern side of the lake, the Loeb Boathouse is the park's high-end restaurant and—though verging on the cliché—a beautiful place to have lunch or just a drink. Tables look out from the restaurant's covered patio over the lake, with incredibly serene views of the trees and parkland around it and the silhouettes of the westside skyline on the horizon. Those brave or energetic enough should rent a rowboat to explore the lake.

⑫ ALICE IN WONDERLAND SCULPTURE

Farther east from the Loeb Boathouse stands a delightfully oversize bronze sculpture of Alice, the Mad Hatter, and the White Rabbit from Lewis Carroll's *Alice in Wonderland*. Like the Frances Hodgson Burnett memorial in the Conservatory Garden and the Hans Christian Andersen Monument near the Conservatory Water nearby, the *Alice* sculpture celebrates an icon of childhood and imagination and brings an element of joy and wonder to the park.

⑬ KERBS BOATHOUSE

In the spirit of childlike wonder, the Kerbs Boathouse is a small café decorated with model boats that sits beside the pond known as Conservatory Water.

The pond is famous for attracting model boat enthusiasts who bring their vessels on weekends and watch them negotiate the waters from the terrace around the edges. It's a whimsical sight and a fun place to sit with a drink and watch the maritime miniatures

⓮ BETHESDA FOUNTAIN

Walk west across the top of Pilgrim Hill and you'll arrive at the grand Bethesda Fountain. The Bethesda Terrace is one of the park's grand landmarks, with terra-cotta and marble colored stonework and stair-cases leading down to the lake. The fountain sits at the top of the terrace, with the *Angel of the Waters* statue rising above it.

⓯ CHERRY HILL

To the west of Bethesda Terrace, Cherry Hill is one of the park's most serene and scenic areas. Named for the cherry trees that pop-ulate the hills and turn it white and pink with blossoms every April, Cherry Hill feels like a clearing in a forest, with views of treetops, greenery, and water in any direction.

⓰ LE PAIN QUOTIDIEN

One of nearly fifty locations in the city, the charming little Pain Quotidien south of Cherry Hill is the perfect place to pause for a drink or a snack, whether it's coffee and a pastry or a hearty bistro-style lunch. While it lacks the grandeur of the Loeb Boathouse, Le Pain has outdoor tables that make dining here feel almost as if the park is your own private garden.

⓱ THE MALL

The grandest and most formal element of the park, the Mall is a long, elegant, tree-lined esplanade that runs all the way from the Olmsted Flower Garden at its southern end to the Bethesda Terrace and Fountain at its northern end. With benches lining either side beneath the trees, it's also the most European-feeling part of Central Park, reminiscent of the oldest gardens in Paris or Florence and a beautiful walk from top to bottom.

⓲ THE CAROUSEL

Just south of 65th Street, the Carousel is one of the park's iconic attractions. There has been an active carousel in exactly this spot of the park since 1871; the current carousel dates to 1908, and although it's in wonderful condition and carefully maintained, the horses show charming signs of age, so a ride on it feels timeless.

19
WOLLMAN RINK

Short of Santa Claus himself dropping down the needle of the Empire State Building, nothing could be quite so perfect a picture of winter in New York than the Wollman Rink. Every winter since 1949 from October through April, the rink has been the city's most popular place to ice skate. Between May and September the 50,000-square-foot space is transformed for the spring and summer months into Victorian Gardens, an amusement park with an old-fashioned feel, with gentle rides like teacups and carousels and classic fairground snacks from ice cream to funnel cake. But nothing is prettier or more romantic than whizzing around the ice with the trees of the park and the flickering lights of the city's skyline around you.

MANHATTAN SKYLINE

As well as casting the most famous architectural shadow in the world, the buildings that shape Manhattan's skyline also tell the story of the city.

ONE WORLD TRADE CENTER is the tallest building in the city and was constructed alongside the National September 11 Memorial and Museum. The tower is visible from far and wide across the city and stands well above even neighboring office buildings of the Financial District. The observation deck on the 102nd floor is panoramic and enclosed by windows, making it a good view to seek out when it's too cold to be in the open air.

THE WOOLWORTH BUILDING was in its day the tallest building in Manhattan. Constructed in 1913, it was one of the country's first skyscrapers and amazingly remains one of the hundred tallest buildings in America. The lobby is ornate and cathedral-like, with vaulted ceilings and mosaic walls, and although you can only see it on one of the Woolworth's paid tours, the basement is an interesting window into the city's history—architectural remnants from the building's restorations are stored here, and there are grand doors that once led directly to the subway.

One of the city's most distinctive landmarks, the **FLATIRON** is a triangular Beaux-Arts building that looks out over Madison Park and has been an icon of New York since its completion in 1902. The building was long occupied by book publishers, and the area still bears signs of its literary heritage with publishers' and agents' offices clustered nearby and the beautiful Rizzoli bookstore a block up Broadway.

Until the Woolworth came along, the **MET LIFE TOWER**—originally built in 1909 to house the offices of Metropolitan Life Insurance—was the tallest building in the world. It now houses, above the Credit Suisse offices, the chic Edition Hotel, whose atmospheric Clocktower restaurant looks out over Madison Park. Try the American Cereal Killer cocktail at the bar adjoining the restaurant; it's an X-rated glass of Cheerio milk served with a striped paper straw.

Nothing is more iconic of New York City than the **EMPIRE STATE BUILDING.** Named for New York State itself, its stacked silhouette and Art Deco facade have made it the most recognizable building in the world. For forty years after its completion in 1931, the Empire State was the tallest building in the world. Even though it has long since lost that distinction, its status as cultural artifact, from King Kong to Andy Warhol and the millions who visit its observation deck every year, is untouchable.

A rival to be the most beautiful example of Art Deco architecture in the city, the **CHRYSLER BUILDING**'s gleaming roof catches the light like nothing else over midtown. Finished in 1930, the Chrysler was New York's tallest skyscraper for just under a year before the Empire State Building went up ten blocks to the south. While there are no tours of the building beyond the ground floor, the Chrysler's golden Deco lobby is the most gorgeous in the city.

The home of the iconic Rainbow Room—as well as the famous "30 Rock" television studios of NBC—**30 ROCKEFELLER PLAZA** is one of the defining buildings of midtown. Its observation deck offers some of the best views in the city, not only because they are panoramic but because both its famous neighboring Art Deco icons—the Empire State and the Chrysler Buildings—are visible from here.

A recent addition to the skyline, **432 PARK AVENUE** is a stark column marking the northern end of midtown and overlooking Central Park. It is the tallest residential building in the world; the second tallest building in the city; and the third tallest in the country.

ISAMU NOGUCHI'S

WALK

The Japanese American sculptor and designer Isamu Noguchi, who lived in New York on and off for half a century and whose remarkable museum is the final destination of this walk, was reported to have attached great importance to experiencing the city by foot, and to have walked frequently from the buzz of Manhattan back to the tranquility of his studio in Queens. Following in his footsteps is not often on a tourist's (or even a local's) agenda, but can introduce you to stunning views of the city that are all too easily overlooked, and some important points in its history. Amid the department stores of Midtown East, Sutton Place and what's colloquially referred to as "Woody Allen's bench" form an oasis of calm looking onto the river. The Cable Car, fantastic as an attraction in its own right, can drop you down into the surreal peace of Roosevelt Island, whose parks and historic buildings feel miles—and centuries—from the metropolis just across the water. And a short walk over the bridge to Long Island City—a vibrant young neighborhood with the Museum of Modern Art's PS1 outpost and nightlife spots like the locals' favorite LIC Bar and the excellent Mexican restaurant Casa Enrique— brings you to two of the city's most interesting monuments to sculpture, in the Socrates Sculpture Park and Noguchi's museum itself.

❶ SUTTON PLACE PARK

Some of New York's greatest treasures can be found in the secret spaces that break away from the unrelenting grid or hide behind the looming architecture of the city. One such treasure is Sutton Place Park, a tree-lined green space tucked alongside one of the city's only private streets, Riverview Terrace in Midtown East. Though

many will know the view from this spot, made iconic by Woody Allen for the bench where he and Diane Keaton sit and watch the sunrise in Manhattan, very few know how to find it. An enclave in a relatively unexplored part of the city—just a short walk from the bustle of Grand Central, the shops of Lexington Avenue, or the U.N. building nearby—Sutton Place is a peaceful corner with spectacular views of the East River, the Queensboro Bridge, Roosevelt Island, and Queens beyond. *Riverview Terrace, New York, NY 10022*

❷ TRAMWAY PLAZA

In the shadows of the Roosevelt Island tram station, Tramway Plaza is another of Midtown's all-too-often overlooked green spaces. With the East River on one side, the traffic of Midtown on the other, and the cable cars swinging above, the park is a surreal kind of urban oasis. In a nod to the cultural allure of Queens across the river, the park plays host to rotating installations of sculptures, which hide among the trees and benches year-round. *Second Avenue between East 59th and East 60th Streets, New York, NY 10022*

❸ ROOSEVELT ISLAND TRAM

The most modern tramway in the world, and the first to be built strictly for public transportation, the Roosevelt Island Tram is one of the great feats of New York engineering and a treat for any adventurous explorer of the city. Opened in 1976, the tramway runs parallel to the Queensboro Bridge and links Midtown East to Roosevelt Island in the middle of the East River. With windows on all sides, each tram car offers incredible views of the city, from Manhattan to Long Island and up and down the river beneath. Originally intended for commuter traffic to and from the developing neighborhoods on Roosevelt Island, these days the cable car is as much tourist attraction as transit, having been made famous by cameo roles in action movies from Nighthawks to Spider-Man. Short of a helicopter ride, it's one of the most novel ways to see the city from above—and, at the price of a Metrocard swipe, it's a lot cheaper! **East 59th Street at Second Avenue, New York, NY 10022**

❹ SMALLPOX MEMORIAL HOSPITAL

Near the southern end of Roosevelt Island are the Gothic remains of the Renwick Smallpox Hospital—the only ruins in the city designated a historic landmark. Dating to 1856, when smallpox was rife and patients warranted isolation in what was then known as Blackwell's Island, the hospital was closed a century after it opened and has been crumbling in a spooky state of disrepair since the 1960s. Visible from Manhattan—particularly when illuminated at night, like a location for a ghostly movie—the hospital is extraordinary to see in person and adds a poignant sense of the city's history to a stroll around an otherwise remote and peaceful island. ***Roosevelt Island, New York, NY 10044***

❺ FOUR FREEDOMS PARK

At the very southern tip of the island, the Franklin D. Roosevelt Four Freedoms Park is one of New York's most perfectly conceived (and least-known) green spaces. Designed by the influential architect Louis I. Kahn in tribute to the former president, a monumental staircase and avenues of trees form a triangle thrusting into the

East River, commanding beautiful and unusual perspectives of the midtown skyline on one side and Long Island City in Queens on the other. Frequented only by Roosevelt Island locals and adventurous walkers, the park is almost always quiet and, like many of Kahn's projects, feels almost religious in its serenity. **Roosevelt Island, New York, NY 10044**

⑥ BLACKWELL HOUSE

An amazing anachronism in the middle of the island, the Blackwell House is all that is left of the private farm that used to occupy Roosevelt Island from its colonization in the seventeenth century onward. Built for James Blackwell, for whom the Island was named until the twentieth century—when, after a brief incarnation as Welfare Island, it was named for Franklin D. Roosevelt in 1973—the farmhouse dates to 1796 and is still surrounded by some of the woodland landscape that separated the house from its farmland. Having served as a home for wardens overseeing the various hospitals and institutions on the island over the years, the Blackwell House is now a community center—and a stunning step back in time. **500 Main Street, Roosevelt Island, New York, NY 10044**

⑦ BLACKWELL ISLAND LIGHTHOUSE

At the opposite end of the island from the Smallpox Memorial Hospital, another construction by the architect James Renwick looks out over the East River toward Upper Manhattan and the Bronx. The Blackwell Island Lighthouse, built in 1872 from rock quarried by inmates at Roosevelt Island's own penitentiary, was active until the Second World War and is one of just eight lighthouses that re-

veal the city's maritime history. While the tower itself isn't open to the public, the green space surrounding the lighthouse offers unique views of the city that few make the trek to see. ***Roosevelt Island, New York, NY 10044***

8 ROOSEVELT ISLAND BRIDGE

The only way for pedestrians and cars to travel from Roosevelt Island to Queens is via the Roosevelt Island Bridge. Uniquely industrial in its look, the bridge is actually spectacular to cross by foot, with vertiginous views across Long Island City and down to the East River below. ***Roosevelt Island, New York, NY 10044***

9 SOCRATES SCULPTURE PARK

A short walk along Vernon Boulevard from the Roosevelt Island Bridge, alongside Rainey Park and its views back toward the island, Socrates Sculpture Park is both a public park and museum. Founded by the sculptor Mark di Suvero in 1986, Socrates is an outdoor space where artists put together long-term exhibitions of sculptures and multimedia installations. With a schedule of exhibitions that run throughout the year, and with events from yoga classes to farmer's markets in the warmer months, the park is a popular space where views of the East River and the Manhattan skyline are made more magical by the extraordinary objects around you. *32-01 Vernon Boulevard, Queens, NY 11106*

❿ THE NOGUCHI MUSEUM

Just a block from the Socrates Sculpture Park, the Isamu Noguchi Foundation and Garden Museum is one of New York's most peaceful places. Open to the public since 1985, the museum was built by Noguchi himself, whose studio had been nearby since 1961. As well as housing a vast permanent collection of Noguchi's sublime sculptures, the museum features a Japanese-style garden with pebbled paths as well as water fountains and sculptures hiding among pine trees and willows. It is hands down one of the most beautiful and serene places to sit and reflect anywhere in the city. With a small bookshop and a café inside, the Noguchi Museum is a lovely end to a journey from midtown—and a fitting tribute to the artist who paved the way. *9-01 33rd Road, Queens, NY 11106*

HOW TO EAT
LIKE A NEW YORKER

Eating like a New Yorker doesn't just mean fancy restaurants and long waits for tables—some of the most authentic New York eats are as iconic of the city's streets as the buildings themselves.

HOT DOG

Of course, there are higher-class iterations of the hot dog on offer here and there (from Shake Shack to Mile End). But the humble New York hot dog should not be underestimated and is a beloved snack of carnivorous locals. From the hot dog carts that dot the streets to institutions like Grey's Papaya, Nathan's, or Feltman's of Coney Island, sausages in buns are everywhere. Eat it like a New Yorker, on the move, with onions and mustard.

PIZZA

New York pizza is thin, crispy, and ubiquitous. Whether you casually pick up a slice from one of the thousands of places around the city, or seek out the very best—Joe's in the West Village, or Paulie Gee's in Greenpoint—the golden rules are the same. Order a plain slice; sprinkle it with red pepper flakes and oregano; and fold it at the crust, so you can hold it in one hand and eat it on the go.

BAGEL

For many New Yorkers, a good bagel is something worth moving to a new neighborhood for. No longer only the preserve of old-school Jewish delis, great bagels can be found all over the city—from Park Slope's anti-toasting

Bagel Hole to creative new chains like Black Seed. Just make sure you're buying them fresh, and not wrapped in cellophane from a bodega counter. Eat it like a New Yorker, with a schmear of cream cheese and a coffee.

COFFEE

Coffee is more commonly available in New York than in any city in the world. So iconic are the classic Greek diner–style takeout cups that the Museum of Modern Art's design store sells porcelain versions of them to use at home. But in a city that indulges every level of caffeinated pretention—from La Mercerie's oat-milk cappuccinos to Bluebottle's slow-drip Japanese cold brew—drinking it like a real New Yorker still means getting your coffee cheap and hot at a bodega, in a paper cup with a flat plastic lid, with a couple of napkins for when you spill it on the steps down to the subway.

DELI SANDWICHES

Sandwiches take many forms around the world; in New York, the classic deli sandwich is served on fresh rye bread and piled so high with pastrami that it takes a practiced hand to eat one without silverware. Some of the city's most famous old-school delicatessens have closed now—the iconic Second Avenue Deli had to move up to Murray Hill, and the Carnegie Deli made famous in Woody Allen's *Broadway's Danny Rose* shut down in 2016—but there are still places to get a real New York pastrami on rye, with the best-known being Katz's on Houston Street. Eat it like a New Yorker, with nothing but mustard and a pickle on the side.

CHICKEN AND RICE

As popular on the city's streets as coffee carts and hot dog trucks, various iterations of the classic street-meat treat of halal chicken and rice dot the blocks of nearly every busy section of Manhattan. The best examples are usually to be found close to the biggest concentration of office workers—the starving hordes of Midtown, Gramercy, and the Financial District—with reliable franchises such as Rafiqi's or Sammy's serving the freshest chicken on beds of the best-seasoned rice and crisp salad.

INTERNATIONAL CUISINE

New York's culinary scene is wonderfully diverse, but you can find its most authentic representations of international cuisine in those neighborhoods scattered around the city that are most densely populated with people from one part of the world or another. Trust the locals over the aesthetics or location of a restaurant, and you'll find your way to the most authentic flavors. Here, we've suggested just one or two standouts from five of the city's best-known culinary enclaves—but use these as starting points to explore these areas, and you'll discover many more restaurants, markets, bakers, butchers, or bubble tea spots that reflect each community's cultural identity.

POLISH

Polish bakeries, butchers, grocers, and restaurants of many kinds dot the neighborhood of Greenpoint—but the most authentic snacks are to be found in restaurants like Pyza, where classic dishes from pierogis and chicken cutlets to potato and beet salads are served on plastic trays, Soviet-era cafeteria-style. ***Pyza, 118 Nassau Avenue, Brooklyn, NY 11222***

CHINESE

Look for the restaurants that are popular with Chinese locals in the Chinatowns of Manhattan and Queens, and you'll find the most authentic meals and the freshest ingredients. The traditional Jewish New Yorker's Christmas Day meal is Peking Duck—one of the best examples of which is at Peking Duck House on Mott Street. *Peking Duck House, 28 Mott Street, NY 10013*

INDIAN

There are concentrations of Indian restaurants in several parts of the city—from Murray Hill (affectionately known as "Curry Hill") to the East Village—but the densest is in Jackson Heights, in Queens. Locals in the know travel to the Jackson Diner for the buffet lunch on weekends, where you can feast on an endless supply of everything from rogan josh to vegetable samosas, and they make dosas fresh to order. *Jackson Diner, 37-47 74th Street, Jackson Heights, NY 11372*

KOREAN

The couple of blocks of lower Midtown East that constitute Manhattan's Koreatown are lined with Korean cafes, bakeries, restaurants, and karaoke places—and, just like in Korea itself, places are often found upstairs rather than in a street-facing storefront. Try the Korean barbecue at Kang Ho Dong Baekjeong. *Kang Ho Dong Baekjeong, 1 East 32nd Street, NY 10016*

RUSSIAN

The neighborhoods of Brighton and Sheepshead Bay, which border Coney Island at the Brooklyn shore, are filled with Russian and Ukrainian markets and restaurants. Try Tatiana, an icon of the Brighton Beach boardwalk, for authentic Russian smoked fish and stroganoff; and the wonderful Tashkent Supermarket, whose vast buffet of prepared Russian, Ukrainian, Uzbek, and Turkish foods, make delightful (if unlikely) picnics for the beach. *Tatiana, 3152 Brighton 6th Street, Brooklyn, NY 11235; Tashkent Supermarket, 713 Brighton Beach Avenue, Brooklyn, NY 11235*

CHELSEA

1. Whitney Museum of American Art
2. High Line (Part 1)
3. Milk Gallery
4. Chelsea Market
5. High Line (Part 2)
6. Galleries
7. Cookshop
8. General Theological Seminary Garden (The Close)
9. Billy's Bakery
10. Momofuku Nishi
11. 192 Books
12. Dia Art Foundation
13. High Line (Part 3)
14. Printed Matter
15. Aperture Foundation
16. Gallow Green at the McKittrick
17. Frying Pan

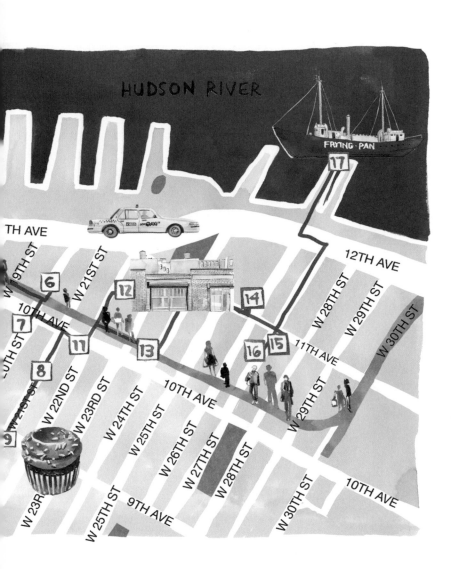

HUDSON RIVER

FRYING·PAN

17

TH AVE

W 19TH ST

6

W 21ST ST

12TH AVE

W 28TH ST

W 29TH ST

12

300

14

W 30TH ST

7

10TH AVE

11

13

15

16

11TH AVE

W 20TH ST

8

W 22ND ST

W 23RD ST

W 24TH ST

W 25TH ST

10TH AVE

W 29TH ST

9

W 26TH ST

W 27TH ST

W 28TH ST

W 30TH ST

10TH AVE

W 23R

W 25TH ST

9TH AVE

The transformation of Manhattan's west side with the creation of the High Line has been remarkable, even by New York's standards, with the once-ramshackle Meatpacking District now a hub of high-end shopping, and the new commercial and residential developments of Hudson Yards breathing life into the long-industrial part of midtown south of Hell's Kitchen. Chelsea, sandwiched between the two, has for decades been one of Manhattan's chicest neighborhoods, with streets of gorgeous brownstones at its eastern side and prestigious art galleries inhabiting former warehouse buildings in the wide blocks that lead west toward the Hudson. The High Line makes exploring Chelsea an absolute joy: a verdant feat of progressive landscaping in its own right, it lets you rise above the streets and negotiate your way happily between the neighborhood's many gastronomic and cultural delights—from the labyrinth of vendors at the Chelsea Market to the largest concentration of major galleries anywhere in the world. (Chelsea comes alive on Thursday nights, when new exhibitions open and eclectic crowds hop from gallery to gallery.) The views from the High Line are difficult to leave; but there are enough lesser-known cafés, shops, and gardens hidden among the prettier blocks in the 20s to make a more adventurous stroll around the neighborhood interesting—from the Theological Seminary's idyllic courtyard to longtime institutions like Billymark's dive bar and the Printed Matter bookshop.

❶ WHITNEY MUSEUM OF AMERICAN ART

One of the great art institutions of New York, the Whitney Museum was established in 1930 and moved into its glorious new loca-

tion on Gansevoort Street in 2015. Designed by Renzo Piano, the new building affords more than fifty thousand square feet of gallery space inside and thirteen thousand square feet of outdoor exhibition space. The museum's permanent collection includes iconic work from Andy Warhol to Alexander Calder and Grant Wood, and the Whitney Biennial—organized every other year with rotating guest curators—displays work from contemporary artists around the world. With views in every direction—out across the city, up the High Line through Chelsea, and over the Hudson River to the west—the building is worth visiting for its spectacular terraces alone. ***99 Gansevoort Street, New York, NY 10014***

❷ HIGH LINE (PART I)

The conversion of a disused industrial railway line into an elevated park in 2009 created one of New York's most popular and enduring landmarks. The High Line runs from the Meatpacking District through Chelsea to Hudson Yards just below Midtown East, and in just a decade has transformed the neighborhoods it passes through. Worthy of a walk from top to bottom, it can be used as a kind of guide for exploring the west side of Manhattan, joining it for its best lookout spots and descending it to enjoy the best of the streets beneath. Designed by the Dutch landscaper Piet Oudolf, the gardens along the walkway are planted with grasses and perennials that are native to the area and inspired by the wilderness that grew here among the abandoned rail tracks. The southernmost portion of the High Line includes some of its most spectacular vistas: start at the Tiffany & Co. overlook, which gives you a picturesque view of the bustling cobbled streets and glamorous renovated warehouse buildings of the Meatpacking District; then walk up through the landscaped gardens to the Diller–von Furstenberg Sundeck, where you can move sliding chairs along the rails of the original train line to a position looking out over the Hudson. Visible to the north, straddling this first stretch of the High Line, is the iconic facade of the Standard Hotel—whose guests are kindly requested not to flash the pedestrians below! **Gansevoort to West 14th Streets, New York, NY 10014**

❸ MILK GALLERY

Cooler, younger, and more fashion- and photography-oriented than the bigger-name galleries in Chelsea, Milk is an exhibition space that also functions as a venue for events from catwalk shows during fashion week to project presentations by students from the city's art schools. Their program of exhibitions is often focused on artists or work with connections to music and popular culture. Stop at Blue Bottle Coffee next door to get a pick-me-up after a snack at Chelsea Market, and see what's on at Milk before you ascend back to the High Line. **450 West 15th Street, New York, NY 10011**

❹ CHELSEA MARKET

A hub for the hungry Manhattanite any time of day, the Chelsea Market is an epicurean's dream: a vast indoor market bringing together vendors of all things edible, from specialty bakers, butchers, fishmongers, and grocers to counters serving delicious food from all over the world. The options are almost overwhelming, with everything from donuts to ramen, coffee to bubble tea, and pizza to Korean BBQ. To refuel for a walk up the High Line, try one of the city's lesser-known champions of Mexican cuisine: Los Tacos No. 1 has an entrance on 15th Street that lets you escape the crowds inside the market and serves some of the freshest and most authentic fish tacos and ceviche tostadas you can find. **West 15th Street at Ninth Avenue, New York, NY 10011**

❺ HIGH LINE (PART 2)

The stretch of the High Line that begins at West 16th Street takes you through the southern end of Chelsea, where the shops and restaurants of the Meatpacking District start to give way to galleries. The passageway between West 15th and West 16th Streets—playfully illuminated with colored lights on the walls and ceilings—is often lined with ice cream carts and sweet food trucks, if you're still in need of a snack after Chelsea Market. At West 17th Street, step down into the Tenth Avenue Overlook, where rows of wooden benches afford great views over the traffic below and you can follow the avenue all the way to the horizon in the distance. As you walk up toward West 20th Street, the urban jungle of architecture becomes more and more varied around the High Line—look out for the fluid curves of Frank Gehry's IAC building to the east of the walkway at 18th Street. ***West 16th to West 20th Streets, New York, NY 10011***

❻ GALLERIES

One of the great pleasures—and traditions, for New Yorkers—of walking around Chelsea is the wealth of galleries found here. The neighborhood has been an epicenter of high-end modern and contemporary art for decades; when Soho became too expensive in the 1980s, galleries migrated to the large factory and warehouse buildings of Chelsea. The area buzzes on Thursday evenings with crowds attending openings of new shows, and on weekends people wander the wide blocks between Ninth and Tenth Avenues from gallery to gallery, either walking off the brunch they've just eaten or working up an appetite for the brunch they're about to have. There are dozens to choose from, but some of the most significant galleries on this stretch include Gagosian, Lehmann Maupin, and David Zwirner, all of which exhibit some of the biggest names in the art world, from

Richard Prince to Liza Lou and Jeff Koons, respectively. ***West 20th to West 23rd Streets between Ninth and Tenth Avenues, New York, NY, 10011***

❼ COOKSHOP

A favorite of gallery-hoppers, Cookshop is a wonderful farm-to-table restaurant with a menu of hearty and seasonal American dishes from pancakes to pork chops. Windows onto Tenth Avenue offer a view of passersby and the High Line and river beyond, and there are tables outside for people-watching in the warmer months. Though it's best known for its brunch, Cookshop is also great for a smaller plate to fuel you for more walking or a feast to celebrate the end of a busy day. A small bar in the front has an excellent cocktail list if you just want to pause with a drink to soak up the Chelsea atmosphere. ***156 Tenth Avenue, New York, NY 10011***

❽ GENERAL THEOLOGICAL SEMINARY (THE CLOSE)

One of the city's best-kept secrets is the Close, the garden within the General Theological Seminary on West 21st Street. The neo-Gothic buildings surrounding the Close, built between the 1820s and 1880s, were designed to recreate the atmosphere of an Oxford college. Though the seminary is an active center of theological education, the gardens are technically open to the public; if the gate on 21st Street isn't open, you can sign in with ID at the seminary's main entrance on Ninth Avenue to gain access. The garden is serene and beautifully landscaped with large trees overhanging lawns and gardens—and sometimes the seminary leaves croquet mallets and deck chairs out on the grass in the summertime. *440 West 21st Street, New York, NY 10011*

9 BILLY'S BAKERY

Before doughnuts, cronuts, and artisanal pizza, cupcakes were the emblematic treats of New York, and Billy's proves that some things transcend the trends of the culinary world. Stepping into Billy's is like stepping back in time to a kitschy 1940s-style kitchen full of bright frosting and quaint desserts. There are all sorts of sweets to choose from— icebox cakes, pies, banana puddings—but the light, fluffy, and delicious cupcakes are what it's famous for. *184 Ninth Avenue, New York, NY 10011*

10 MOMOFUKU NISHI

An interesting meeting of cuisines and flavors, Momofuku Nishi is—loosely speaking—an Italian restaurant with Asian influence. Part of the Momofuku empire of restaurateur David Chang, it offers classic Italian dishes with unusual touches—tagliatelle with crispy pork skin or baked eggs with Sichuan tofu—

alongside a range of meat and fish dishes that bring in flavors from both cuisines. *232 Eighth Avenue, New York, NY 10011*

⑪ 192 BOOKS

A small shop with a giant impact, 192 is the neighborhood's most beloved independent bookstore. While most of its selection is comprised of new fiction, nonfiction, and poetry books, the store's location in the heart of Chelsea's gallery district means it keeps a well-curated selection of art monographs as well. The iconic storefront windows have enticed readers into the shop since 2003, and it's also a popular venue for readings and events, which frequently draw big names in literature and the arts. *192 Tenth Avenue, New York, NY 10011*

⑫ DIA ART FOUNDATION

Dia Art Foundation is a major presence in New York, for both its space in the city and its beautiful Riggio Galleries upstate in Beacon. Once housed in a multistory building farther east on 22nd Street, Dia moved into its new home in the former Alcamo Marble building in 2015. With a mission to represent cutting-edge contemporary art, the foundation shows a mixture of work from its permanent collection—which mostly includes conceptual, minimalist, and abstract art of the 1960s, 1970s, and 1980s—and newly commissioned projects. The galleries in Chelsea have a busier program than the galleries in Beacon, where installations are often on longer-term view. Plans to expand exhibition space and reintroduce the Dia bookstore to

Chelsea are in development. *535 West 22nd Street, New York, NY 10011*

⓭ HIGH LINE (PART 3)

The upper section of the High Line differs in character from its southern counterparts, in large part because of the architecture surrounding it. As the walkway winds through Chelsea's gallery district, walls and windows close in on either side, so pedestrians feel as if they're walking right through the buildings of the neighborhood. The lawn at 23rd Street is a serene and surreal resting place, an oasis of green floating between the brick walls of warehouses on either side, and the Falcone Flyover, which runs from 25th to 27th Streets, focuses foot traffic into a narrower path overhung with extraordinary lush greenery from magnolias to sassafras. Look out for the 26th Street spur, where the path juts out over the street below and you can rest on wooden benches and watch the city go by. The High Line concludes just a few blocks farther north, among the gleaming new residential towers and malls of Hudson Yards and Thomas Heatherwick's towering Vessel sculpture. *West 23rd to West 34th Streets, New York, NY 10011*

⓮ PRINTED MATTER

Founded in 1976 by a group of artists—Sol LeWitt and Ingrid Sischy among them—Printed Matter was established with the mission of producing and selling artist's books and other creative projects in which artists retained control of every aspect of production. The organization grew over the decades, and now—in its latest space on the western edge of Chelsea—it operates as a nonprofit, working both to publish books and to sell interesting publications that

reflect the world of contemporary art. Its store is unique, with a vast selection of books, zines, catalogs, and ephemera, much of which you simply cannot find anywhere else. Work from major publishers is mixed in along with a good selection of rare and collectible art books, but the majority are independently produced limited editions from artists around the world. The store also hosts events and readings aimed distinctly at the younger side of New York's art scene. ***231 Eleventh Avenue, New York, NY 10001***

⓯ APERTURE FOUNDATION

Focused exclusively on photography, Aperture is a prestigious not-for-profit organization that exhibits and publishes work from the great masters to the brightest new names of the genre. Part gallery space, part bookstore, and part publishers' offices, Aperture's space on West 27th Street is always exciting to visit, with rotating exhibitions of work on the walls and a constantly changing selection of photo books on display. Keep an eye out for the office cat, who makes his way onto the gallery floor from time to time. **547 West 27th Street, New York, NY 10001**

⑯ GALLOW GREEN AT THE McKITTRICK

The elegant red-brick McKittrick Hotel building is actually not a hotel but the setting for the celebrated theater company Punch Drunk's site-specific, interactive production Sleep No More—a noir interpretation of Shakespeare's Macbeth that allows the audience to explore the set and engage with the actors. Whether or not you go for the show, the building's other secret is a spectacular rooftop bar known as the Gallow. Enclosed within a rustic-feeling cover but open on all sides during the warmer months, the Gallow offers great views of a part of the city seldom seen from above—and has a mean cocktail list to boot. **542 West 27th Street, NY 10001**

⑰ FRYING PAN

If you prefer to test your sea legs over your vertigo, the Frying Pan is the place to go for views and drinks after a day of walking around Chelsea. Set aboard a retired Coast Guard's lightship dating to 1929, the Frying Pan is one of the neighborhood's liveliest watering holes. The boat's various decks were converted into bars, sitting areas, and a kitchen, so visitors can feast on salty bar snacks

and enjoy drinks overlooking the Hudson. Open from May through October—and on especially warm days during the off-season—the Frying Pan is best visited early evening, so you can find a seat before it gets too crowded and watch the sunset over New Jersey across the river. *Pier 66 at Hudson River Park, Twelfth Avenue at West 26th Street, New York, NY 10001*

PARKS OF NEW YORK

With Central Park, Manhattan boasts one of the most beautiful and most famous parks of any city in the world. But there is much more to New York's public green spaces, many of which are just as beautiful but less frequently visited by tourists and warrant walks all their own.

PROSPECT PARK

The biggest park in Brooklyn, Prospect Park was landscaped by Calvert Vaux and Frederick Law Olmsted, also the designers of Central Park. A little wilder and less obviously manicured than its Manhattan counterpart, Prospect Park can feel like a country oasis, with hills, lakes, waterfalls, woodlands, and acres of open fields. But it's also large and varied enough that you can discover se-

cluded spots, like the Vale of Cashmere—a series of circular clearings with fountains almost hidden up a path near the Grand Army Plaza entrance—or the woods that run around the lake, where small benches look out over the water beneath pagodas. Smorgasburg, the fabulous food market that began on the Williamsburg waterfront (see page 146), operates here on Sundays from April through October at Breeze Hill on the Lefferts side, so you can reward yourself after a hike through the park with a scenic picnic lunch.

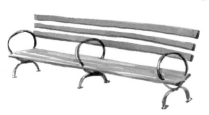

McCARREN PARK

With a pool, a skate park, a running track, and all kinds of sports fields, Mc-Carren Park is a hive of activity, particularly in the warmer months. Bordering the Brooklyn neighborhoods of Williamsburg and Greenpoint, McCarren is also one of the best parks for people-watching, with an endless parade of locals from hipsters to Hasidim strolling the paths, snacking on the benches, and sunbathing on the fields. One of the city's biggest greenmarkets operates on Saturdays year-round in the southwestern corner of the park, and nearby, the Green Dome community garden is the perfect oasis of flowers in which to enjoy the bounty of a market stroll.

McGOLRICK PARK

One of Greenpoint's hidden treasures, McGolrick is a small rectangular park with tree-lined avenues running between beautifully planted green spaces. Surrounded by near-perfect blocks of turn-of-the-century townhouses and with the classical Shelter Pavilion at its center, the park has a quiet European feel to it—something complemented by the many Polish residents in the neighborhood. The park also features several monuments and has commissioned temporary public artworks by local artists, such as the *Ziemia* sculpture by Martynka Wawrzyniak—a clay orb nestled in a native plant meadow, referencing the pre-urban wilderness of the area.

VAN CORTLANDT PARK

Bigger than Central Park and wilder than Prospect Park, Van Cortlandt is the Bronx's most beautiful green space and offers true escape from the city. A popular place for trail running and mountain biking, the parkland feels less landscaped and more like upstate countryside than anywhere else within the five boroughs. At more than one thousand acres, Van Cortlandt also accommodates a golf course and space for a lot of sports—including cricket, the beloved game of many locals of Caribbean and British communities. Van Cortlandt has eleven cricket fields—more than anywhere in the entire country—and hosts everything from lazy pickup games to organized league matches, so go with a picnic hamper on a Sunday in summer and enjoy this most civilized pursuit of the commonwealth in all its glory.

FLUSHING MEADOWS

The largest public park in Queens, Flushing Meadows is one of the city's most extraordinary green spaces, with a host of amenities including playgrounds, a lake, and two museums. Just blocks from the New York Mets' baseball stadium, and incorporating the Arthur Ashe stadium and the site of the annual U.S. Open tennis competition, the park is also a hub for sports—and even hosts local cricket games on weekends in the summer. The site of the 1964 World's Fair, the park still retains monuments from the occasion, including the iconic Unisphere sculpture at the apex of the park's grand promenades. Seek out the eerie remains of the New York State Pavilion, another remnant from the fair; it's been abandoned for more than fifty years, but is maintained by a preservation-minded community and is amazing to walk around and imagine in its heyday.

WEST VILLAGE

1. Washington Square Park
2. Blue Note
3. Air's Champagne Parlor
4. Comedy Cellar
5. Minetta Tavern
6. Joe's Pizza
7. Murray's Cheese
8. Cherry Lane Theatre
9. Church of St. Luke in the Fields Garden
10. Grove Court
11. Little Owl
12. Buvette
13. Fat Cat
14. 55 Bar
15. Smalls
16. Stonewall Inn
17. Three Lives & Co. Bookstore
18. 93 Perry Street
19. Bookmarc
20. Magnolia Bakery
21. Abingdon Square Park
22. Corner Bistro

One of few older parts of the city where the streets go off-grid, the West Village has long been the heart of New York's bohemia. Its meandering roads and beautiful townhouses, while picturesque (and priceless) now, have housed significant emblems of cultural rebellion, from the speakeasies that defied prohibition to underground jazz clubs, landmarks of progressive literature, and cornerstones of the gay rights movement. As well as harkening to the city's past, the erratic footprint of the Village's streets also makes it a neighborhood full of surprise and discovery, with curious lanes and alleyways to explore, parks decorating corners and squares, and courtyards and gardens hidden behind pretty brick walls. Although it's one of New York's most heavily touristed areas, the West Village is also a densely residential part of town, which is what allows it to retain its charm; Hitchcock set Rear Window here, and in spite of the hum of visitors walking its streets, the place still has the same sense of quiet closeness in which Jimmy Stewart's character kept an eye on his neighbors. Between the high-end boutiques of Bleecker Street and restaurants like Via Carota and Tartine, the Village today has a gentrified and European feel to it; but the bohemian spirit is still there, in the louche cocktail bars, jazz and comedy clubs, and the cobbled streets themselves.

❶ WASHINGTON SQUARE PARK

With the exception of Central Park uptown, Washington Square is New York's best-known and most frequently visited park. Surrounded by some of Manhattan's oldest and most elegant buildings—including a landmarked and carefully preserved row of Greek Revival townhouses on the northern side—the park is also the city's most European-feeling public space, with curving paths, landscaped flower beds, a grand fountain at the center, and the famous Washington Square Arch framing the glorious view of Fifth Avenue uptown. The arch was modeled after Paris's Arc de Triomphe and installed here in 1892, though the rest of the park dates back to the mid-nineteenth century. Having been the epicenter of downtown Manhattan society in one way or another since its creation—from the well-to-do Greenwich Village socialites of the 1850s to the hippies who gathered here in the 1960s—the park today is still as vibrant as ever, as popular with locals as with tourists. ***Washington Square, New York, NY 10012***

❷ BLUE NOTE

Although younger than many of its peers—it opened in 1981—the Blue Note Jazz Club is one of the city's most prestigious music venues. The program of performers extends into other genres, from hip-hop to R&B, which distinguishes it from some of the more purist clubs, but the Blue Note's reputation is founded on having hosted the very biggest names in jazz, from Dizzy Gillespie to Dave Brubeck and the Modern Jazz Quartet. ***131 West 3rd Street, New York, NY 10012***

❸ AIR'S CHAMPAGNE PARLOR

With a lush interior of marble, velvet, and gold, everything about a visit to Air's feels suitably decadent. Cozily lit and intimate, the bar is always lively, with a sophisticated downtown crowd and a delicious menu of luxurious bar snacks to complement the champagne, from caviar to cheese boards, charcuterie, and oysters. Far from feeling exclusive, however, the mission of Air's is to make champagne more approachable; their extensive and rotating list of champagnes, available by the glass or by the bottle, focuses on broadening horizons and showing people other sides of champagne beyond its typical celebratory pop. No matter how accessible it might be, though, nothing feels quite as glamorous as sitting in the window, sipping champagne, and watching the well-dressed West Village crowds. *127 Macdougal Street, New York, NY 10012*

❹ COMEDY CELLAR

The iconic glittering sign has been beckoning people downstairs to the Comedy Cellar since 1982. One of the world's most famous comedy clubs, it has played host to every huge name in stand-up comedy and remains a training ground for up-and-coming comedians from all over the country. Jon Stewart, Sarah Silverman, Judah Friedlander, and Dave Chappelle have all performed here; Jerry Seinfeld even went on to film some of his movie *Comedian* here; and the club's famous entrance was cemented in the public imagination in the introduction sequence to Louis C.K.'s television series *Louie*. Stop in for a glimpse of that famous red-brick wall, no matter who's in the spotlight in front of it. *117 Macdougal Street, New York, NY 10012*

❺ MINETTA TAVERN

The Minetta Tavern is old-school New York. Beneath another of the most iconic neon

signs in the city, the restaurant has been serving classic steaks, burgers, and chops since 1937. With a distinctly Old World feel—wood-paneled and muraled walls, tin ceilings and checkered tiled floors, and waiters with waistcoats and their shirt sleeves rolled up—Minetta belongs absolutely to the charming old streets of the West Village outside. Taken over in 2009 by the successful local restaurateur Keith McNally (who is also responsible for other jewels in New York's culinary crown, such as SoHo's Balthazar), Minetta continues to be a carnivore's paradise: a wonderful place to enjoy steak with a strong glass of wine or, for the initiated, a whiskey. **113 Macdougal Street, New York, NY 10012**

❻ JOE'S PIZZA

Even New Yorkers don't consider themselves New Yorkers until they've folded a slice of Joe's pizza and eaten it over a paper plate in Father Demo Square, the leafy triangular park across the street. For many, the taste of hot, fresh pizza and the sights and sounds of the intersection at Sixth Avenue is home. Keep it simple—a regular slice or one with pepperoni is all you need—and watch out for the pigeons. **7 Carmine Street, New York, NY 10014**

❼ MURRAY'S CHEESE

A turophile's delight, Murray's is—like a slice from Joe's or an H&H bagel or a hot dog from a cart in Central Park—an emblem for every New Yorker's taste buds. Founded in 1940 by Murray Greenberg and certainly the best cheese shop in the city, Murray's stocks an incredible and ever-changing range of cheeses from around the world: alpine triple creams, Spanish manchegos, hard blue English cheddars, and soft cheeses from Wisconsin produced only in

limited quantities every year. What's more, it helps you learn to enjoy them, too. The vast display cases inside are mouthwatering (you can sample anything you like), and the store hosts tastings and pairing courses in a charming space upstairs for the more adventurous cheese lovers. They have a to-go menu of sandwiches, too, if you want to bring something with you for the walk. **254 Bleecker Street, New York, NY 10014**

❽ CHERRY LANE THEATRE

Behind beautiful red-arched doors on one of the West Village's prettiest streets, far from its cousins in Midtown, the Cherry Lane Theatre is the city's oldest off-Broadway theater. The tiny performance space—which seats just sixty people—has been a home for independent and increasingly prestigious productions since 1924. Emerging from its awning into the lamplight of Commerce Street is one of the most romantic things you can do in the city. **38 Commerce Street, New York, NY 10014**

❾ THE CHURCH OF ST. LUKE IN THE FIELDS GARDEN

Through an easily missed gate in the red-brick wall that runs along this block of Hudson Street lies one of the city's prettiest gardens. Maintained by the episcopal church, which was established here in 1821, the gardens have been developed through the centuries into a magical series of verdant spaces, joined to one another by charming paths that wind around the church and its adjoining school. The Barrow Street Garden has an English feel, with a flagstone path surrounded by leafy hedges and ivy-clad old trees, and the Rectory Garden is planted with roses and colorful flower beds that attract legions of butterflies. Benches are placed here and there throughout, and the garden is seldom busy, making it a beautifully peaceful place to step away from the noise of the Village streets. ***487 Hudson Street, New York, NY 10014***

⑩ GROVE COURT

Tantalizingly visible between the railings of a cast-iron fence—and behind a charmingly hand-painted sign that reads "Private court—no trespassing"—lies Grove Court, one of the West Village's most gorgeous enclaves. A row of six picturesque little townhouses with shuttered windows looks onto the cobbled court, with ivy climbing the red-brick walls and a small manicured garden in the center. The court has been private since the houses were built in the 1850s, and the homes, though small, are understandably some of the most desirable in the city. There are few more picturesque places in Manhattan. **13 Grove Street, New York, NY 10014**

⑪ LITTLE OWL

While the food at Little Owl is some of the best around—with a lovely menu of Mediterranean dishes and a famously good burger at brunch on the weekends—it's the view that makes a table here so hard to come by. The restaurant's large plate-glass windows look out onto one of the Village's prettiest corners, where tree-lined Grove Street bends toward Hudson Street, with historic townhouses across the street in either direction. You'll also see crowds of tourists gathering here on the opposite corner; Little Owl occupies the ground floor of the building that appeared as the exterior of the characters' apartments on *Friends*. **90 Bedford Street, New York, NY 10014**

⑫ BUVETTE

Popular with the city's European crowd, Buvette opened in 2011 with the look and feel of a bistro you'd find in Paris (where they opened a sister location in 2012). Cozy and warm during the winter and with a charming garden overhung with trees in the back that's perfect in the summertime, Buvette has an incredible wine list and an inventive menu of small but hearty plates. It's a particularly romantic place to break from a walk for sustenance. *42 Grove Street, New York, NY 10014*

⓭ FAT CAT, ⓮ 55 BAR & ⓯ SMALLS

Clustered within a block of one another near Christopher Park and Seventh Avenue South are some of the city's oldest and greatest jazz clubs. While each has its own vibe—Fat Cat for a livelier and younger crowd, 55 Bar for a more bluesy vibe, and Smalls for the most intimate performances you can experience— these three in particular continue to define the character of the neighborhood and its historic connection to jazz music. Pick one and settle in early with a good table for the night, or hop from club to club for a taste of the different sights and sounds of the Village jazz scene. *75 Christopher Street, 55 Christopher Street, and 183 West 10th Street, New York, NY 10014*

⓰ STONEWALL INN

The Stonewall Inn is one of the most culturally significant of New York City's landmarks and a place of pilgrimage for people from all over the world. The site of the Stonewall riots—considered to be one of the defining events in the gay liberation movement and the history of Western sexual politics—the bar was the most important venue

for gay and lesbian New Yorkers in the late 1960s. Though half of the original building was taken over by neighboring properties when the bar closed after the riots in 1969, the half that remains looks largely unchanged from the original facade and is registered not only as a New York City Landmark but as a National Historic Landmark and National Monument. **53 Christopher Street, New York, NY 10014**

⓱ THREE LIVES & CO. BOOKSTORE

A beloved neighborhood bookstore, Three Lives & Co. has occupied the charming red-doored storefront on the corner of West 10th Street and Waverly Place for more than fifty years. The shop squeezes a tremendous selection of new fiction, nonfiction, and classics into its cozy space and hosts readings or launch events every week. It's a lovely place to browse; the staff are known for holding strong opinions and being forthcoming with their recommendations. **154 West 10th Street, New York, NY 10014**

⓲ 93 PERRY STREET

Hidden inside an arched doorway on Perry Street is a courtyard that looks so perfect it could be from the set of Hitchcock's *Rear Window*. Though not strictly private (like Grove Court, page 87), the lamp-lit little space leads exclusively to the single building that adjoins it and is decorated with plants and garden furniture by the residents. For the bold explorer it's worth a look to see one of the most charming spaces in the Village, evocative of a peace and privacy inaccessible to most of the city. ***93 Perry Street, New York, NY 10014***

⓳ BOOKMARC

The New York outpost of fashion designer Marc Jacobs's bookstore chain is every bit as chic as you'd expect. The selection of books is geared toward the taste of a fashion-forward New Yorker, with only the very coolest illustrated books on art, fashion, photography, and pop culture on display. The shop frequently hosts events and book launches, when crowds steam up the small storefront windows and prosecco is served in ice cold cans. Jacobs bought the space when the former tenant, a used bookstore, was forced to close down in the face of rising rents; the idea behind Bookmarc was to recognize a bookstore's importance to the community and keep it alive, even when the neighborhood is as expensive and fashionable as Bleecker Street. ***400 Bleecker Street, New York, NY 10014***

⓴ MAGNOLIA BAKERY

The pretty blue awning of the Magnolia Bakery on Bleecker Street has been a beacon for those with a sweet tooth since the bakery opened in 1996. Always a local favorite, their cupcakes have been as iconic an emblem of New York as the humble hot dog since *Sex and the City*'s Carrie Bradshaw memorably tucked into one on a bench outside the store. Though the cupcakes live up to the hype, those in the know look for Magnolia's mind-blowing cups of banana pudding—small tubs of the sweet filling you might find in an old-fashioned banana cream pie. ***401 Bleecker Street, New York, NY 10014***

㉑ ABINGDON SQUARE PARK

At the very end of Bleecker Street, Abingdon Square is one of the city's smallest parks. With benches lining the perimeter, shaded beneath the trees surrounding a war monument, it's also one of the prettiest, and a lovely place to rest from the bustle of the West Village's busiest streets. On Saturdays, a greenmarket occupies the corner of Hudson and West 12th Streets nearby. ***Hudson Street at Bleecker Street, New York, NY 10014***

㉒ CORNER BISTRO

A classic West Village burger joint, the Corner Bistro has illuminated the corner of West 4th and Jane Streets with its comforting neon sign for more than fifty years. Too nice to be a dive and too low-key to be fancy, the Corner Bistro became famous in the 1970s for serving one of the best burgers in the city, made from a blend of beef sourced directly from the Meatpacking District a few blocks south. ***331 West 4th Street, New York, NY 10014***

EAST VILLAGE

E 23RD ST

3RD AVE

2ND AVE

E 22ND ST

1

E 20TH ST

3

2

3RD AVE

E 19TH ST

2ND AVE

W 18TH ST

1ST AVE

E 23RD ST

E 18TH ST

E 17TH ST

E 16TH ST

E 15TH ST

1ST AVE

13

FDR DR.

EAST RIVER

FDR DR.

9

10

E 12TH ST

RUSSIAN & TURKISH
SINCE 1892
BATHS
HEALTH CLUB

E 9TH ST

11

AVENUE C

1ST AVE

E 8TH ST

E 11TH ST

E 12TH ST

12

E 10TH ST

AVENUE D

AVENUE A

1ST AVE

E 6TH ST

AVENUE B

E 9TH ST

AVENUE C

E 10TH ST

AVENUE D

FDR DR.

13

E 5TH ST

14

E 7TH ST

E 8TH ST

4TH ST

2ND AVENUE A

E 3RD ST

15

E 2ND ST

Though much gentrified now—and often maligned by longtime locals for having evolved beyond recognition from the dangerous New York of old—the East Village still bears signs of its history of punk rock and poetry, with lively street life and the kind of bars, restaurants, and venues that keep the neighborhood young. The culture here is flavorful and eclectic, with the recent arrival of "little Tokyo" joining long-established Ukrainian, Jewish, Irish, and Hispanic communities to make each block different from the next. Walking down into the East Village from Gramercy is a good way to appreciate the character of the neighborhood, as things get rougher and more energetic as you move southeast of Union Square. Grittier than its genteel counterpart on the west side, the architecture here is a mixture of townhouses and apartment buildings that show their age—but, dotted with a surprising number of parks and green spaces from Tompkins Square to the gardens of Alphabet City, the neighborhood is picturesque in a way all its own.

❶ GRAMERCY PARK

A tantalizing tease for passersby and an exception in an otherwise universally accessible city, Gramercy Park is the only private park in Manhattan. First laid out in the 1830s and made private for residents of the buildings surrounding the park in 1844, Gramercy Park has occupied one of the city's most beautiful squares for almost two centuries and gave this elegant neighborhood its name. While the park itself is accessible only to residents, the square around it is open thoroughfare and makes for one of the prettiest strolls anywhere in Manhattan. Beautiful buildings line all four sides of the park, ranging from ivy-covered mid-nineteenth-century townhouses to austere Art Deco apartment buildings and the chic Gramercy Park Hotel

(whose restaurant, Maialino, serves some of the most delicious Italian food around). The park is unlocked to the public for one day only every year: Christmas Eve. **_Gramercy Park between East 20th and East 22nd Streets, New York, NY 10010_**

❷ BLOCK BEAUTIFUL

Famously referred to in an interiors magazine in 1909 as the "block beautiful," the stretch of East 19th Street between Irving Place and Third Avenue still lives up to the name today. A uniquely eclectic mix of architecture distinguishes the block from the most pristine of Gramercy's other gorgeous streets. Though most of the buildings date to a similar period—the mid-nineteenth century—they represent a charming mixture of shapes, sizes, styles, and colors. Townhouses with wood shutters and bricks painted in pastel tones sit beside Gothic facades, Tudor-style apartment buildings, and even a Flemish carriage house. **East 19th Street between Irving Place and Third Avenue, New York, NY 10010**

❸ 71 IRVING

Irving Coffee has been a staple of the neighborhood since 1996. Busy from morning to night, it's a charming café with famously good coffee and a menu of snacks from breakfast pastries to bagels, soups, and sandwiches. Its many tables and counter seats are crowded with Gramercy locals, from artsy students of the nearby School of Visual Arts to sophisticated media professionals tapping away at their laptops—which makes it both a great spot to refuel for a walk around the city and a wonderful place to people watch and get a sense of the area's character. **71 Irving Place, New York, NY 10003**

❹ UNION SQUARE

One of Manhattan's historic squares, Union Square has been a hub of the city in every sense for more than a century. The subway station beneath unites almost every subway line in the city, and the square itself is a meeting point for the busiest areas downtown—with the shops of Fifth Avenue to the west, the businesses of Flatiron and Gramercy to the north, Greenwich Village and NYU to the southwest, and the East Village to the southeast. Among the trees, benches, and lawns of the park are statues commemorating, among others, George Washington, Abraham Lincoln, and, at the center of the park, Victoria, the goddess of victory. Originally laid out with grand intentions, these days its many monuments are obscured by the bustle of its street life and the shops and restaurants nearby. Crowds gather to sit and eat or play chess at the southern side of the park, and a greenmarket operates in the western and northern sides of the park every Monday, Wednesday,

Friday, and Saturday throughout the year. *Union Square between East 14th and East 17th Streets, New York, NY 10003*

❺ THE STRAND

The Strand has been in operation for almost one hundred years and is simply the city's most beloved bookstore. Of the nearly fifty bookshops that made up New York's original Book Row—the literary district that in the 1920s and 1930s defined the section of Fourth Avenue south of Union Square—the Strand is the sole survivor. The Strand moved to its present location in the 1950s and established itself as the city's most prolific bookseller, carrying not only tens of thousands of used books but also brand new titles in every category, from fiction and poetry to art monographs and rare books. With floor after floor of books, the shop is perennially busy, hosts book launches and events regularly, and is a New York institution. *828 Broadway, New York, NY 10003*

❻ GRACE CHURCH

One of the city's most significant architectural landmarks is easily missed on a quiet stretch of Broadway south of Union Square. An early commission by the architect James Renwick Jr.—who also designed another notable New York landmark, St. Patrick's Cathedral in Midtown—Grace Church is a small masterpiece of French Gothic Revival architecture, built almost entirely of marble cut by the inmates of the Sing Sing penitentiary upstate. Its exterior is stunningly intricate, and its ornate interior is flooded with light that filters through a remarkable stained-glass window. **802 Broadway, New York, NY 10003**

❼ COOPER UNION

Founded in the mid-nineteenth century by the industrialist and philanthropist Peter Cooper, the Cooper Union for the Advancement of Science and Art is one of New York's most prestigious schools of higher education. Since its establishment in the 1850s, the school has expanded, and a large new building occupies the entire block between East 6th and 7th Streets across Third Avenue. Its original building—the Foundation Building at Cooper Square—is an icon of the East Village, a grand Italianate hall built in brownstone that presides over the northern end of the Bowery just south of Astor Place. Classes are held here, and a program of cultural events takes place in the Great Hall—also the site of a famous 1860 speech by

Abraham Lincoln, which many believe was significant in his path to the presidency. The Cooper Triangle, a small park immediately in front of the building's grand entrance, is a surprisingly tranquil place to pause in the middle of such a busy part of the city. **30 Cooper Square, New York, NY 10003**

❽ LITTLE TOKYO

Much of the Japanese community in New York is focused in the East Village, and the stretch of East 9th Street heading east from Third Avenue is known affectionately as Little Tokyo. As well as a plethora of hairdressers (an area of Japanese expertise in New York) and a grocery store (the Sunrise Mart, upstairs near the corner of Stuyvesant Street), there are some remarkable restaurants and bars here. The Village Yokocho is a charmingly informal yakitori place with a long counter facing the chefs' hot grills and a secret cocktail bar called Angel's Share through a door in the corner; Hasaki is a sophisticated restaurant with some of the best sushi downtown; Cha-an is a cozy tea shop with delicate sweet and savory snacks to accompany carefully brewed Japanese teas; and Decibel is a lively subterranean sake bar where you're encouraged to graffiti the walls while you eat and drink. **East 9th Street between Second and Third Avenues, New York, NY 10003**

❾ ST. MARK'S CHURCH IN-THE-BOWERY

Though the building itself is the second oldest church in New York, the site of St. Mark's Church in-the-Bowery is the oldest place of continuous religious worship in the city. What makes this church special beyond its history, though, is that its location in the East Village has given it a connection to a very particular kind of local culture. In 1966, the publicly funded Poetry Project established its home here, bringing together figures from countercultural communities such as the Beats and artists of the New York School who had long made downtown Manhattan their stomping grounds. William S. Burroughs read here, as did Allen

Ginsberg and John Ashbery; Patti Smith has read and performed music here, as have Philip Glass and Arthur Russell; and Robert Lowell and Yoko Ono have numbered among the many artists who have taken part in the annual marathon poetry readings, which have been hosted here every New Year's Day since 1974. In addition to being a busy and active church, St. Mark's in-the-Bowery continues to be a venue for local literary, music, and dance events. **131 East 10th Street, New York, NY 10003**

❿ MOMOFUKU NOODLE BAR

The first restaurant opened by local superstar chef David Chang—who now operates a small empire of restaurants under the Momofuku brand—Momofuku Noodle Bar serves the best ramen in the city. Always lively, the restaurant attracts everyone from locals to tourists and even admiring Japanese chefs from other kitchens nearby. The dining room is warm and engaging, and the menu includes other treats, from pork dumplings to succulent fried chicken—but Momofuku is best enjoyed simply, with a restorative bowl of ramen at the counter. *171 First Avenue, New York, NY 10003*

⑪RUSSIAN AND TURKISH BATHS

For more than 125 years, the scent of eucalyptus has wafted down the block of East 10th Street between First Avenue and Avenue A. The Russian and Turkish Baths—affectionately known to locals as "the tenement spa"—have drawn people from around the city to steam in the Turkish steam room and soak in the Russian sauna in the basement of this townhouse since the 1890s. The baths are co-ed and perfectly reflect the atmosphere of the East Village, with an eclectic clientele that mixes shabby older types with trendy youngsters. There's something amazing about emerging refreshed from a quick schvitz to go right back into the heart of the East Village. *268 East 10th Street, New York, NY 10009*

🄬 TOMPKINS SQUARE PARK

Established in 1850, Tompkins Square Park encapsulates the spirit and history of the East Village. At once charming and scruffy, the park attracts a mixed crowd, from the younger generation of trendier gentrifiers to aging punks, hippies, and a cast of questionable characters who give the neighborhood its edge. With historic statues, lawns to sunbathe and picnic on, a greenmarket on weekends, and spaces for performances or readings set up by the local community, the park has plenty to do and see. But the true treat is the dog run in the northeast corner of the park, where locals come—with canine companions or otherwise—to talk, people-watch, and sip coffee to soothe their hangovers. *East 7th to East 10th Streets between Avenues A and B, New York, NY 10009*

⓭ MAST BOOKS

Mast sells a careful selection of art, design, fashion, and photography books from this small and charming storefront on the outskirts of Alphabet City. The shop carries new and used books, including some very rare and hard-to-find art and photography volumes, as well as a lot of titles with the kind of countercultural edge associated with the East Village. The store holds events for readings and launches, and often curates small exhibitions of printed matter alongside the books; one recent display collected books and papers from the library of the late design guru Jim Walrod. *72 Avenue A, New York, NY 10009*

⓮ COMMUNITY GARDENS OF ALPHABET CITY

Some of the city's unsung treasures, community gardens are scattered around much of the East Village and Lower East Side. Maintained by the community, each garden has its own character, whether oriented toward growing vegetables and flowers for green-thumbed locals

or a beautifully land-scaped tranquil retreat from the busy streets. There are more than a dozen gardens between Tompkins Square Park, Avenue D, and Houston Street, but three of the prettiest fall in a row on East 6th Street—the Creative Little Garden, the Sixth Street and Avenue B Community Garden, and the amazing 6BC Botanical Garden—and are lovely places to stroll or pause to recharge among the flora. *East 6th Street between Avenues A and C, New York, NY 10009*

⓯ NUYORICAN POETS CAFE

An iconic facade of Alphabet City, with its mural depicting silhouettes of people lining up to take part, the Nuyorican Poets Cafe is a long-standing cultural institution of the East Village. A nonprofit organization dedicated to the arts, the café is—like the jazz cafés of the West Village or the Apollo Theater in Harlem—a venue tied to the voices of its community. Regular performances include poetry readings and hip-hop performances, as well as dance, comedy, and theater productions, almost all of which reflect the eclectic cultural and political heritage of the neighborhood. *236 East 3rd Street, New York, NY 10009*

LOCATION LOCATION LOCATION

Most people around the world learn about New York City from TV shows and movies—it's the most recognizable backdrop in the world, and from Travis Bickle's taxi to Carrie Bradshaw's stoop it has been the setting for more iconic moments on the big (and small) screen than anywhere else. Here are a few you might pass by without even knowing it.

FRIENDS APARTMENT BUILDING
The building on the corner of Bedford and Grove Streets in the West Village, which also houses the wonderful Little Owl restaurant, is the exterior of the *Friends* characters' homes—though, as locals will tell you with a shade of bitterness, there's no way any apartment in this building is as big or light and airy as they suggest on the show.

WOODY AND DIANE'S BENCH
In the 1979 film *Manhattan*, Woody Allen and Diane Keaton watch the sun come up from a bench facing the East River and the Queensboro Bridge, in Sutton Place Park in Midtown East.

CARRIE BRADSHAW'S APARTMENT
The most famous stoops in the city belong to numbers 64 and 66 Perry Street, which shared the role as the *Sex and the City* heroine's home.

YOU'VE GOT MAIL PARK

At the climax of one of New York's classic rom-coms, Joe and Kathleen meet at the 91st Street Garden and Crabapple Grove, one of the prettiest sections of Riverside Park overlooking the Hudson on the Upper West Side.

SEINFELD'S DINER

Tom's Restaurant in Morningside Heights near Columbia is the diner whose facade was made famous in the long-running sit-com *Seinfeld*.

MR. ROBOT APARTMENT

At 217 East Broadway, just a block away from Seward Park on the Lower East Side, is the exterior of the apartment that was home to Oscar-winning actor Rami Malek's character in the tech-conspiracy drama *Mr. Robot*.

DO THE RIGHT THING WAY

Spike Lee shot the entirety of the iconic 1989 movie *Do the Right Thing* on a single block of Brooklyn's Bedford-Stuyvesant neighborhood, on Stuyvesant Street between Quincy Avenue and Lexington Avenue. The block is now named for the movie.

THAT TABLE FROM *WHEN HARRY MET SALLY*

It's been thirty years since Meg Ryan pounded the table with Billy Crystal, and people still make the pilgrimage to Katz's Delicatessen on Houston Street—not just for the pastrami sandwiches and the hot dogs, but to "have what she was having."

NOLITA &

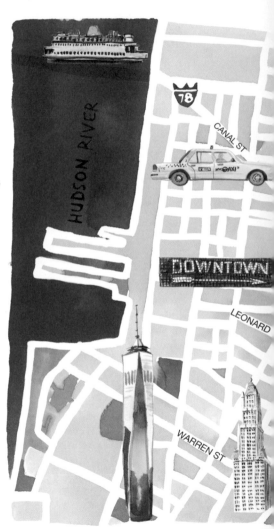

HUDSON RIVER

78

CANAL ST

NYC TAXI

DOWNTOWN

LEONARD

WARREN ST

CHINATOWN

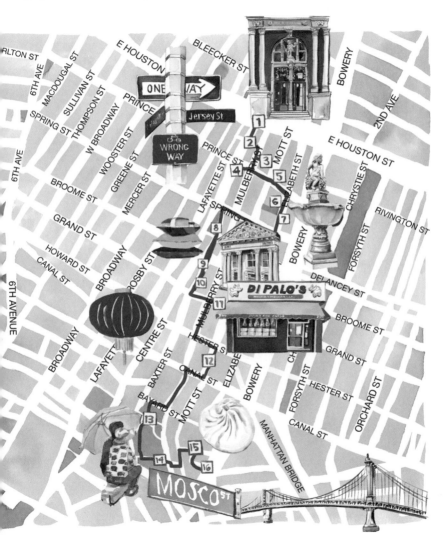

For a century after the immigration boom of the 1880s, the neighborhoods of Little Italy and Chinatown were among the densest and poorest immigrant communities in the country; tenement neighborhoods where Italian was the language most often heard on the blocks below Houston Street and Chinese dialects on the streets north of Canal. In recent decades, as the art, cool, and commerce have leaked in from the surrounding neighborhoods of SoHo, NoHo, and the Lower East Side, the area has become its own flavorful enclave. The roots of its past are still there, from the Cathedral on Prince Street to the delicatessens and pizzerias around Grand and Mulberry Streets, and in the Chinese markets, restaurants, spas, and specialty stores that line the labyrinth of streets by the Bowery and mark your entry into Chinatown. But mixed among them now are galleries, bookstores, cafés, and young designers' boutiques that cater to the chic downtown New Yorker and make these narrow, pretty streets worth exploring. Framed by historic landmarks—the glorious Puck building at one end, the Police Building in the center, and Columbus Park, the site of the city's notorious Five Points, at the other—the area feels at once young and old, contemporary and anchored in tradition.

❶ THE PUCK BUILDING

Presiding over Houston Street with one of the most recognizable facades in the city, the Puck Building counts among downtown Manhattan's greatest architectural and cultural landmarks. Constructed in the late nineteenth century, during a period when Romanesque Revival architecture defined many of the city's most historic blocks, its red bricks and green details have housed a succession of New York's cultural institutions, from magazines and printing presses to universities. The building takes its name from the

satirical *Puck* magazine, which had its offices here from 1887 until it closed in 1918; two gilded statues of the Shakespearean character by the sculptor Henry Baerer decorate the entrance on Lafayette Street and the corner of Houston and Mulberry Streets. ***295 Lafayette Street, New York, NY 10012***

❷ JERSEY STREET

Tucked between the Puck Building and the Mulberry Street branch of the New York Public Library, this block of Jersey Street is one of the more picturesque treasures of Nolita. Dating to the 1820s, this humble alleyway offers not just respite from the traffic of Lafayette Street but also the most archetypal downtown views, such as the nineteenth-century storefronts of Crosby Street to the west and the quaint St. Michael's Russian Catholic Byzantine Church—with a pastoral churchyard and the red-brick row houses of Mott Street behind it—to the east. *Jersey Street between Lafayette and Mulberry Streets, New York, NY 10012*

❸ BASILICA OF ST. PATRICK'S OLD CATHEDRAL AND CHURCH

Until the larger Gothic St. Patrick's arrived in Midtown in 1879, the Basilica of St. Patrick's Old Cathedral was the seat of the Roman Catholic Archdiocese of New York. Built in 1809, Old St. Patrick's has been an icon of Little Italy for more than two centuries—both as an epicenter of the community that defined so much of this neighborhood's history and as the setting for memorable scenes in Italian American cinema, from Francis Ford Coppola's *The God-*

father to Martin Scorsese's *Mean Streets*. The church-yard is bounded by the prettiest red-brick wall in the city (along the Prince Street side of which a flea market operates on week-ends); and although the cathedral's main entrance is on Mott Street, there are thoughtfully made peep-holes opened by latches in wooden doors on the Mulberry Street side where passersby can peer in for a glimpse of the otherwise private tree-lined cemetery. **260–64 Mulberry Street, New York, NY 10012**

❹ McNALLY JACKSON

Now the flagship of a small local empire—with related stationery stores on Mulberry Street and West 8th Street, and other locations for books in Williamsburg and the South Street Seaport—the McNally Jackson bookstore on Prince Street is both the best independent bookshop in the city and a popular idling ground for many a downtown flâneur. With a large collection of fiction books organized by the nationality of their author, brilliant magazine racks stocked with the most obscure publications, and a strong selection of art books from both major and independent publishers, the store draws a uniquely cool crowd of literati and fashionistas. The café on the ground floor is a lovely (if lively) place to sit, read, and observe the Nolita crowd passing by St. Patrick's through the window. *52 Prince Street, New York, NY 10012*

❺ CAFE GITANE

This French Moroccan café on Mott Street has long been the place to be seen in Nolita. With a chic and cozy interior, blue-jacketed waitstaff, and a menu of pastries, tagines, and citrons-pressés straight out of a Parisian bistro, Gitane draws crowds of shopping tourists on weekends and louche locals for lazy breakfasts during the week. But as much as it is a place to be seen, Gitane is a wonderful place to people-watch: with outdoor tables facing the Basilica and windows onto the busy intersection at Prince Street, it's an ideal spot to take in the charming architecture and fashionable throngs of the neighborhood. *242 Mott Street, New York, NY 10012*

❻ ELIZABETH STREET GARDEN

An unlikely sight amid the crowded shops and row houses of Nolita, this charming quasi-Italianate garden runs from Mott Street to Elizabeth Street, just below Prince Street. In 1990 the garden was leased by the adjacent Elizabeth Street Gallery, whose owner landscaped

the garden as we know it today and installed the eccentric collection of furniture, sculptures, and objets that sit among the trees and lawns. Open to the public (for now, at least, while the city debates tentative plans to construct affordable housing here), the garden is a beautiful place to sit—perhaps with a drink from nearby Gimme! Coffee—and enjoy the rare privilege of quiet green space downtown. *Elizabeth Street between Prince and Spring Streets, New York, NY 10012*

❼ LOVELY DAY

One of the establishments that defined the character Nolita has today, Lovely Day is a Thai fusion restaurant with a shabby-diner-chic feel, which moves seamlessly from the perfect hangover-cure iced latte and light lunch to romantic dinners and cocktails in the downstairs dining room and bar. Local foodies and fashionistas fight over the red leather booths inside; but the best table is out front, where you can observe a slow stream of trendy traffic up and down the boutique-lined block and the Elizabeth Street Garden across the street. *196 Elizabeth Street, New York, NY 10012*

❽ LIEUTENANT PETROSINO SQUARE

This little tree-lined space is, despite its name, one of the most perfect triangles for people-watching in the city—particularly from the benches facing the buzzing Swiss restaurant Cafe Select, the graffiti-strewn buildings on Lafayette, or the iconic downtown Mexican haunt La Esquina. Originally known as Kenmare Square, the park was renamed in 1987 for Joseph Petrosino, a police officer who was hugely influential in the gang-crime heydays of the late nineteenth and early twentieth centuries; the plaque at the park's entrance commemorating his achievements is a stark reminder of this neighborhood's complex history. *Lafayette Street at Cleveland Place, New York, NY 10012*

❾ CLIC

This chic French storefront and gallery, owned by the founder of the clothing brand Calypso, Christiane Celle, has illuminated the windows of a beautiful early-twentieth-century building on the corner of Centre and Broome Streets since 2008. The shop carries a carefully curated selection of collectible art books, beautiful photographic prints, and eccentric furniture, like their ever-present and exceptionally soft sheepskin ottomans, and frequently hosts book signings and other cultural events with a Europhile bent. **255 Centre Street, New York, NY 10013**

❿ THE POLICE BUILDING

This extraordinary Beaux-Arts building on the western cusp of Little Italy served as the headquarters for the New York City Police Department from its construction in 1909 until 1973. Converted into luxury apartments in the 1980s and home to one of the most expensive residences in the city (the "dome" apartment on the top), it's still referred to affectionately by locals and realtors alike

as the Police Building. It's private, so exploring the interior is impossible without knowing a resident there; but the building itself—with its majestic facades and copper-domed pediment—is a grand testament to a bygone age, when the architecture of the city's administration reflected its power. **240 Centre Street, New York, NY 10013**

⑪ DI PALO'S

In the heart of Little Italy, amid the touristy restaurants and gift shops, Di Palo's remains one of the few great authentic Italian delis. Since 1925 its windows have been lined with Parma hams and wheels of cheese, and customers have taken a ticket and waited their turn at the pasta and cold cuts counters. With a tasteful mix of imported and domestic foods, as well as essentials for the Italian American pantry, from anchovy oil to cheese graters, Di Palo's is both a historic attraction for visitors and an invaluable resource for locals. **200 Grand Street, New York, NY 10013**

⓬ MARKETS OF MOTT STREET

Just a few blocks from the prosciutto and red-checkered tablecloths of Little Italy, the stretch of Mott Street that runs from Hester Street down to Canal Street feels a world apart. Unchanged for decades and immersed in the sights, sounds, and smells of Chinatown, this block of fishmongers, butchers, poultry shops, and grocery stores is a kaleidoscopic parade of Chinese delicacies. Crowds swarm around crates of live shellfish, cabinets of dried herbs and spices, windows hung with Peking ducks, baskets of exotic fruits, and nose-to-tail ingredients for only the strongest of heart. A treasure trove for the adventurous cook, these markets are also an amazing spectacle for passersby. **Mott Street between Canal and Hester Streets, New York, NY 10013**

⓭ COLUMBUS PARK

There may be no clearer emblem of New York City's capacity to evolve than Columbus Park. Once the site of the original Five Points—the stomping ground of the characters made famous in Scorsese's *Gangs of New York* and an area contested for more than a century by Dutch, Irish, and Italian immigrants—the park today is a serene hub of the Chi-

nese community. Surrounded by the taller buildings that border the Financial District and the curving row houses of Mulberry Street, the park is protected from the noise and bustle nearby. Older neighbors practice tai chi here at dawn, and families gather to clean and prepare produce from the markets of Chinatown. The beautiful pavilion at the northern end of the park is unique and occupied most often by locals playing mahjong in the afternoons and singing Cantonese opera in the evenings. ***Mulberry Street at Bayard Street, New York, NY 10013***

⓮ MOSCO STREET AND THE FIVE POINTS

This short and unassuming street at the southern tip of Chinatown is not only one of the steepest hills in all New York, but it is also one of the only surviving remnants of the original Five Points, the infamous slum that defined the desperate and violent reputation of the city for much of the nineteenth century. At the Mott Street corner is the Roman Catholic Church of the Configuration, the oldest Catholic Church building in the city; at the Mulberry Street end is Columbus Park. The road itself is the last remaining stretch of the old Cross Street, the rest of which has long been buried under the developments of Tribeca, the Financial District, and Chinatown; it was renamed Mosco Street in 1982 after the local community activist Frank Mosco. ***Mosco Street between Mott and Mulberry Streets, New York, NY 10013***

⓯ JOE'S SHANGHAI

Doyers Street is one of a handful of curved streets in Manhattan and, with the connecting Pell Street, part of the most authentic corner

of Chinatown, mixing classic haunts like Nom Wah Tea Parlor with noodle kitchens and other eateries catering more to Cantonese locals than tourists. Joe's Shanghai is an exception, drawing locals and visitors to the city in equal measure to its large communal tables; it's famous for serving the best soup dumplings in the city. *9 Pell Street, New York, NY 10013*

⑯ LIN SISTER HERB SHOP

Situated on an otherwise unremarkable block on the Bowery, Lin Sister is an Old World holistic Chinese pharmacy of sorts for ancient herbal remedies. Colorful boxes of mysterious medicines line the shelves, and behind the counter is an entire wall of beautiful wooden drawers; inside each drawer is an herb, powder, leaf, or other such ingredient ready to be mixed into a cure for almost any kind of ailment. *4 Bowery, New York, NY 10013*

ART IN THE STREETS

Between the galleries in Chelsea and the Lower East Side, Museum Mile uptown and the storied studios of SoHo downtown, New York is a city of art and a city for artists. For eagle-eyed walkers (and those who know where to look), the city's streets are a gallery unto themselves, too.

On the corner of West 55th Street and Sixth Avenue stands a colorful iteration of Robert Indiana's **LOVE** sculpture. Indiana originally created the design for a MoMA Christmas card; the statue has been here since 1971.

Running alongside the public Carmine Street pool in the West Village is a charming **MURAL BY KEITH HARING**, which he painted here in 1987. Although not the best known of Haring's public works in the city, it is the most easily accessible and at the same time often overlooked.

One of the city's most iconic sculptures, the **CHARGING BULL**— also known as the Wall Street Bull—has stood on the cobbles of Bowling Green since 1989. Although often interpreted as a critical commentary on capitalism (particularly in light of the *Fearless Girl* statue, which once stood facing the bull in defiance and has now been moved to the Stock Exchange nearby), its creator, Arturo Di Modica, intended it as a monument to the strength of the city's financial district.

Two striking cubes have decorated Manhattan's streets since the 1960s: Bernard Rosenthal's Alamo, familiarly known as the **ASTOR CUBE**, which has stood at Astor Place since 1967, and Isamu Noguchi's *Red Cube*, which has added a pop of color to the financial district since 1968. You can spin the one at Astor Place, but not Noguchi's red one!

RECLINING FIGURE, a piece by the famous British sculptor Henry Moore, has floated in the Paul Milstein pool within the modernist courtyard of Lincoln Center since 1965.

On Greene Street in SoHo, laid into the concrete of the street itself, is Francoise Schein's **SUBWAY MAP FLOATING ON A NY SIDE-WALK**, a stainless steel map installed in 1985 that reimagines the MTA's subway system as a part of a living organism.

An entire family of whimsical miniature bronze sculptures decorates the platforms of the subway at 14th Street and Eighth Avenue. The pieces—which comprise Tom Otterness's **LIFE UNDERGROUND**—have inhabited the station since 2004 and give the platforms a Through the Looking Glass feel.

The giant digital clock visible from Union Square, on the facade of the building on the corner of Fourth Avenue and East 14th Street, is in fact a work of art titled **METRONOME** by Kristin Jones and Andrew Ginzel. Its playful sequence of flickering digits has been confounding visitors since its installation in 1999.

LOWER EAST SIDE

1 New Museum

2 Sara D. Roosevelt Park

3 Russ & Daughters Cafe

4 Tenement Museum

5 Essex Street Market

6 The Fat Radish

7 Dimes

8 Metrograph

9 Cactus Store

10 Seward Park

11 Ice & Vice

12 Henry Street Settlement

13 Doughnut Plant

14 Clinton Street Baking Co.

15 Hamilton Fish Park

Still synonymous with New York cool, the Lower East Side is the part of Manhattan that is the most eclectic in character. Bordered by Chinatown, Nolita, and the East Village, and with historically significant Jewish and immigrant populations, the neighborhood is downtown's most vibrant area and at the same time retains many of the landmarks and cultural traditions of its past. Synagogues, settlements, churches, and tenement architecture point to its varied and multicultural history, while bars, markets, cinemas, and pioneering restaurants reflect its continually youthful energy. Crowds of Chinese locals occupy Sara Roosevelt Park on weekend afternoons, playing mahjong beneath the shade of parasols, while fashionable visitors pass through from cafés to boutiques. A densely residential area, the Lower East Side's quiet streets and local parks are a joy to explore and somehow escape the frenetic busyness of the neighborhoods that surround it. Galleries, from major dealers to smaller independents, have opened locations here within walking distance of the New Museum.

❶ NEW MUSEUM

Founded in 1977 and moved into its stunning present location on the Bowery thirty years later, the New Museum is New York's only museum devoted exclusively to contemporary art. Its distinctive building, whose silhouette resembles an asymmetrical tower of stacked blocks, was designed by the Pritzker Prize–winning Japanese architecture firm SANAA to allow for exhibition spaces of varying shapes, dimensions, and levels of light. Continuing its progressive mission within the extraordinary space, the museum's program has seen exceptional large-scale installations from young artists such as Carsten Höller and Chris Burden alongside more formal shows of paintings by artists from Chris Ofili to Elizabeth Peyton. With a small café and bookstore on the ground floor and a terrace around

the seventh-floor Sky Room with panoramic views of downtown Manhattan, the museum is an amazing experience for the art or the architecture alone. ***235 Bowery, New York, NY 10002***

❷ SARA D. ROOSEVELT PARK

One of the city's busiest parks, Sara D. Roosevelt Park is a long promenade of pathways, parklands, and playgrounds that marks the transition from Nolita to the Lower East Side. The park runs all the way from Houston Street at its northern end to Canal Street to the south and borders on several different surrounding neighborhoods. Lower East Side kids play basketball on the courts at the top; tourists and fashionistas take breaks from shopping in Nolita's boutiques on benches alongside Chrystie and Forsyth Streets; and groups of older Chinese people play mahjong or practice ballroom dancing at the bottom. And right in the middle of the park, just below Delancey Street, is the Pit, the city's official bike polo grounds, where you can sit and watch hardy hipsters swinging mallets from fixed-gear bicycles on the concrete. It's a great place to sit with a drink and people-watch to get a sense of the buzz of the Lower East Side. **Houston Street to Canal Street between Chrystie and Forsyth Streets, New York, NY 10002**

❸ RUSS & DAUGHTERS CAFE

With gleaming white counters, cozy booths, and an appetizing menu of knishes, latkes, pastrami, schmaltz, bagels, pickles, and more smoked fish than you can imagine, Russ & Daughters Cafe is a contemporary take on a classic Jewish deli. The sit-down café opened in 2014, exactly one hundred years after its sister establishment—the tiny but legendary deli of the same name, and a New York institution—opened on East Houston Street just a few blocks away. **127 Orchard Street, New York, NY 10002**

❹ TENEMENT MUSEUM

One of the city's truly unique institutions, the Tenement Museum operates tours of two restored historic tenement buildings that serve as windows into the social, economic, and architectural history of the Lower East Side. As a hub of the city's immigrant population for more than 150 years, the neighborhood saw thousands of people living in extraordinary conditions, often with multiple families sharing the same amount of space afforded to just one by today's real-estate expectations. In addition to the tours, the museum also has a wonderful gift shop with a great collection of books on New York's history. **103 Orchard Street, New York, NY 10003**

❺ ESSEX STREET MARKET

The Essex Street Market is one of the city's great food halls and a perfect reflection of the diversity of the Lower East Side. A market of food vendors has existed around this site since 1940 and over the decades has grown to cater to more and more tastes and cultures as the neighborhood has evolved. In 2019 the market moved from its historic hall into a new modern space in the Essex Crossing development across Delancey Street, gaining more space for more vendors. Latin American grocery stores stocking imported Mexican and Ecuadorian products share the space with Italian butchers, Jewish delis, Japanese fishmongers, French bakeries, coffee shops, and gourmet cheese stores. *88 Essex Street, New York, NY 10002*

❻ THE FAT RADISH

Behind a dark and industrial exterior, the Fat Radish is a warm, inviting, and rustic restaurant serving British-inspired farm-to-table food and lavish, fruit-forward, creatively named cocktails. Considering that the Fat Radish is one of the city's trendier restaurants, it is in some ways remarkably uncool: the service takes itself very seriously, the food is resolutely seasonal and healthful, and the atmosphere is more old-fashioned than you would expect of a restaurant with its reputation in such a chic neighborhood. But therein lies its magic; Fat Radish is a people-watching scene, and one with amazing food worthy of the crowds. *17 Orchard Street, New York, NY 10002*

❼ DIMES

An impossibly cool and deceptively inventive restaurant, Dimes is a hip spot that draws a consistently beautiful and fashionable crowd to its colorful little space on the east end of Canal Street. The erratic and delicious menu seemingly combines a health-conscious and vegetable-forward California approach with a carnivore's appetite and brings together American, Mexican, and Mediterranean influences—from acai bowls to spicy BLTs. Beyond a place to eat and drink, it's a place to see and be seen. *49 Canal Street, New York, NY 10002*

❽ METROGRAPH

Set inside an anonymous-looking brick building, Metrograph has quickly established itself since opening in 2016 as the city's coolest indie movie theater. Designed with a clean, retro aesthetic, Metrograph is more art house than mainstream, with a program of international movies, higher-end concessions like truffle popcorn and Japanese candy, and a small shop carrying screenplays and film books upstairs. Everything about the space is beautiful, from the dimly lit auditoriums to the bars and restaurant. You don't need to see a movie to get a drink or a snack here; it's a fun place to sit with a refreshment and absorb the artier faction of the Lower East Side. *7 Ludlow Street, New York, NY 10002*

❾ CACTUS STORE

A seasonal pop-up outlet of a successful Los Angeles garden store, the Cactus Store, tucked into a nook off of Essex Street, feels delightfully incongruous among the gritty blocks around East Broadway. A Japanese-inspired pebbled courtyard with ferns climbing the gray concrete walls and benches sitting among sculptures leads to a small greenhouse filled with cactuses and succulents of seemingly infinite varieties. All are for sale and accompanied with detailed instructions for care in the harsh New York climate. **5 Essex Street, New York, NY 10002**

⑩ SEWARD PARK

Seward Park has been at the heart of the Lower East Side's community for more than a century—it was the first municipally funded playground in the country when it opened in 1902—and continues to reflect the eclectic mix of cultures that defines the area. The park is below the magnificent Forward Building, the former offices of the local Forward (formerly the Jewish Daily Forward) newspaper, which is now converted into beautiful apartments. Chinese neighbors practice tai chi around the fountain and in the playgrounds early in the morning, and the Hester Street Fair, which brings food and arts and crafts stalls to the park weekly from April through October, epitomizes the cooler and younger side of the neighborhood. *Canal Street and Essex Street, New York, NY 10002*

⓫ ICE & VICE

Ice & Vice serves unusual flavors of ice cream, sorbet, and frozen yogurt. Billing themselves as "experimental," the shop combines flavors and textures you won't find anywhere else—all with a cheeky sense of humor. Past flavors have included Nuts of Wrath (with marcona almonds and grape Kool-Aid jam), Movie Night (with popcorn, raisins, and chocolate), and Pork Your Melons (with honeydew, prosciutto chips, and a balsamic reduction)—perfect treats to take to the park. *221 East Broadway, New York, NY 10002*

⓬ HENRY STREET SETTLEMENT

Like the Tenement Museum, the Henry Street Settlement preserves and embodies a fascinating part of downtown New York's history. Founded by the humanitarian Lillian Wald, and housed in a row of pristine nineteenth-century buildings, the settlement's mission since 1893 has been to serve the community, with programs coordinating outreach in everything from education and healthcare to the arts. But even if you're not a resident of the neighborhood, the settlement is interesting to visit; the buildings at 263, 265, and 267 Henry Street are among the best-preserved period townhouses in the city, and The House on Henry Street, a permanent interactive exhibition in the headquarters at 265, explores the history of the Lower East Side and the trials and tribulations of its poorer immigrant communities. *265 Henry Street, New York, NY 10002*

⓭ DOUGHNUT PLANT

The Grand Street location is the original outpost of this revered doughnut chain, which is consistently among the city's most popular. More experimental than most, Doughnut Plant creates flavors that go beyond the usual, with fruit, flower blossoms, and nuts joining the more traditional ingredients. Their doughnuts come in different styles—yeast or cake, circular or square—and often riff on other desserts, from red velvet to carrot cake and even crème brûlée. *379 Grand Street, New York, NY 10012*

⓮ CLINTON STREET BAKING CO.

Pancakes, pancakes, pancakes. Clinton Street Baking Co. has counted among the most popular brunch spots in the city for nearly twenty years, with lines of people waiting patiently around the block. The menu is extensive, with everything from pastries to huevos rancheros; but the real draw here are the pancakes, which are perfectly puffy and come served with fresh blueberries or chocolate chips. *4 Clinton Street, New York, NY 10002*

⓯ HAMILTON FISH PARK

A hidden gem of the Lower East Side, Hamilton Fish Park is a beautiful neighborhood park year-round and a sublime paradise in the summer. In addition to playgrounds, avenues of benches shaded by trees, basketball courts, and the city's only outdoor squash court, the park's major draw is the Olympic-sized pool, which is open from May through September every year. Surrounded by deck chairs and plenty of space for lounging on towels before or after a swim, and framed by two gorgeous nineteenth-century red-brick pool houses, the water itself is beautifully maintained and cleaned daily. The atmosphere is so joyous that stepping into the park feels like leaving the city and taking a beach vacation. And even if you're not in the mood to swim, the benches and picnic tables around the park are lovely places to relax with a snack and unwind after a long day of exploring. **128 Pitt Street, New York, NY 10002**

BRIDGES OF NEW YORK

It's easy to forget when you're in the midst of it that New York is a city of islands. Only the Bronx is part of mainland New York State; Manhattan and Staten Island float alone, Brooklyn and Queens are on Long Island, and the many smaller islands—Roosevelt, Liberty, Ellis, Governor's, Randall's, and City Island, among others—are surrounded by the various rivers, harbors, and bays around the city. The bridges that connect these various parts of the city to one another are essential to the way people navigate and experience the city.

The most famous bridge in the city is also the oldest: completed in 1883, the **BROOKLYN BRIDGE**, is one of the most beautiful suspension bridges in the world. Its tall steel arches are as iconic of New York as the skyline, and its unique wooden-slatted walkways are the most pleasant way to cross the East River—and afford stunning views of New York Harbor and the Statue of Liberty from the middle. (Cyclists beware, though: the slats make for a bumpy ride, and its popularity means the paths are always busy with foot traffic.) The bridge connects the financial district in downtown Manhattan to downtown Brooklyn and the official buildings surrounding Borough Hall, so you can use a stroll across it to explore two of the city's smaller parks. City Hall Park, on the Manhattan side, is an ornate tree-lined garden adjoining the mayor's offices at City Hall; sit and read a book by the Jacob Wrey Mould Fountain, just as the great writer Jack London used to do in his vagabond days. Descend on the Brooklyn side at Cadman Plaza, pick up roasted nuts or fresh popcorn from the food carts at the bridge's exit, and enjoy them in the park near the Brooklyn War Memorial—with beautiful Brooklyn Heights and the start of our Brooklyn Riviera walk (see page 152) just around the corner.

The **MANHATTAN BRIDGE,** which was built in 1912, is less scenic than the Brooklyn Bridge just to the south—but has the advantage of offering views of the Brooklyn Bridge from its walkway. Carrying traffic, pedestrians, subway trains, and a bicycle path, the Manhattan Bridge is one of the busiest in the city. You can join the bridge near the end of our Brooklyn Riviera walk in Dumbo (whose name is an acronym for Down Under the Manhattan Bridge Overpass). On the Manhattan side, the bridge descends into one of the busiest parts of Chinatown, where you can find some of the most authentic Chinese food just a block or two from the bridge's exit—try Great

NY Noodletown around the corner on the Bowery for their famous noodles and suckling pig, or double back and experience the hectic Chinese markets in the arches beneath the bridge itself.

Completed in 1909, the **WILLIAMSBURG BRIDGE** is the second oldest bridge in the city and was built at a time when transportation for goods and workers was required between the growing city and Brooklyn's industrial waterfront neighborhoods. These days, the bridge may be the "coolest" bridge in the city by virtue of connecting consistently hip and desirable neighborhoods: it spans from the nightlife and markets of the Lower East Side to the restaurants and retail of South Williamsburg. If leporine connections are your thing, you can grab coffee or a wonderful brunch at

Rabbithole on Bedford Avenue, around the corner from the bridge's exit in Brooklyn; or take an evening walk over to Manhattan and seek out the charming Japanese restaurant called the Rabbit House on Forsyth Street, just a short block away from where the bridge lets out on Delancey Street.

The **ED KOCH QUEENS-BORO BRIDGE,** also built in 1909, is one of the great architectural icons of the city. Dwarfing the three bridges over the East River to the south, it spans from Midtown East to Long Island City in Queens, passing

over Roosevelt Island. In spite of being less conventionally beautiful than the Brooklyn Bridge, the Queensboro is just as much a focus of popular culture, having played cameo roles in everything from Woody Allen's *Manhattan* and the Spider-Man movie to novels like *The Great Gatsby* and *Charlotte's Web*. For those with a sweet tooth, the bridge on the Manhattan side is close to the Midtown locations of Serendipity and Magnolia, two of the city's most famous dessert spots; and on the Queens side, the famous Tom Cat bakery is a few blocks south of the bridge in Long Island City. And anyone afraid of heights can see Roosevelt Island via the bridge without venturing into the cable car (see page 48).

The **VERRAZZANO-NARROWS BRIDGE,** which connects Staten

Island to Brooklyn, was the longest bridge in the world when it was completed in 1964. Although it's been eclipsed on the world stage since then, it remains the longest, tallest, and most heavily trafficked bridge in the city—and is an astonishing sight. The bridge connects the residential waterfront neighborhoods of Dyker Heights and Bay Ridge in Brooklyn with Short Acres and Arrochar on Staten Island; interestingly, each side also features a historic fort, with Fort Hamilton on the Brooklyn shore and Fort Wadsworth across the Narrows. The only time you can set foot on the bridge is during the New York City Marathon, which closes the bridge every year for thousands of runners. The rest of the year, you have to resort to driving over the bridge to enjoy the phenomenal views from its upper deck—or you can stroll along the boardwalks on either side of the Narrows and appreciate the bridge from below.

NORTH BROOKLYN

1. South Williamsburg Ferry Terminal
2. Marlow & Sons
3. Domino Park
4. Grand Ferry Park
5. Oddfellows Ice Cream Parlor
6. East River State Park
7. Artists & Fleas Williamsburg
8. Kinfolk
9. Wythe Hotel
10. Du's Donuts
11. Chez Ma Tante
12. Word Bookstore
13. Homecoming
14. Paulie Gee's
15. The Brooklyn Barge
16. WNYC Transmitter Park
17. Sweetleaf Coffee
18. Polka Dot

Twenty years ago, the idea of any part of Brooklyn beyond Coney Island's Wonder Wheel being as famous as Manhattan would've seemed extremely unlikely. But the evolution of Williamsburg in recent decades has seen the area grow from industrial wasteland to hipster stronghold and beyond, to become one of the city's best-known neighborhoods and a blueprint for contemporary urban cool. While the gentrification—and yuppification—of the area has made it harder for the kind of one-off boutiques, pop-ups, and parties that defined its hipster regeneration, Williamsburg and its neighboring Greenpoint still demonstrate an incredible cultural range, where independent stores and bastions of a deeply rooted Polish community mix with high-end chains and Michelin-starred restaurants. To get the most out of the neighborhood means to appreciate both, from a beer in a red cup at the Brooklyn Barge to a cocktail overlooking the city at the rooftop of the Wythe Hotel. Often overlooked by visitors, who crowd the L and G trains and flock to the stores and nightlife of Bedford and Manhattan Avenues, is the area's marvelous waterfront; both South Williamsburg and Greenpoint are stops on the East River Ferry route, and using the parks and pathways that run up the river as ways into the neighborhoods can lead to the most enjoyable and authentic exploration of what they have to offer.

❶ SOUTH WILLIAMSBURG FERRY TERMINAL

South Williamsburg is the second stop on the northbound East River Ferry service, which sets off from Wall Street in Manhattan and stops first in Dumbo on the Brooklyn side. The landing here was redeveloped in the early 2000s and the wooden deck is lined with benches facing the river. It is a lovely place to sit and take in the juxtaposition of the area's industrial docks to the south, Manhattan across the water, and the Williamsburg Bridge to the north. **440 Kent Avenue, Brooklyn, NY 11249**

❷ MARLOW & SONS

An institution of South Williamsburg long before the fancy redevelopments reached this far down Kent Avenue, Marlow & Sons is a comforting restaurant with a deceptively elegant menu. Along with its sister restaurant, Diner, which occupies the iconic dinette space on the corner of the same block, Marlow serves decadent and wonderful food disguised with bohemian ease. The dishes, from fresh oysters and country paté to their famous brick chicken, are simple but perfectly prepared and accompanied by fantastic cocktails and wines. The day-lit front room, with the feel of a country kitchen, has a coffee bar and pastries for those on the go, while the back is darker, warmer, and more rustic. The Marlow empire extends to Marlow & Daughters, a selective nose-to-tail butcher and delicatessen on the next block. **81 Broadway, Brooklyn, NY 11249**

❸ DOMINO PARK

In 2010, the hearts of many nostalgic Brooklynites were broken when the city announced a proposed redevelopment of the beloved Domino sugar refinery into apartments. The dark-brick factory, with

its tall chimney and iconic yellow sign, had been a beacon of the Williamsburg waterfront since 1882 (though it ceased operating as a refinery in 2004). The silver lining, however, is the beautiful Domino Park, which now runs along the river in front of the new building complex. Retaining elements of the industrial space's architecture—from columns and machinery taken from the refinery's interior to the steel cranes over the elevated walkway that runs parallel to the East River—the park has opened up to the public a whole new stretch of the waterfront and filled it with lawns, benches, a dog run, and other scenic areas, all with stunning views of the Williamsburg Bridge and the Manhattan skyline. *River Street from South 5th Street to Grand Street, Brooklyn, NY 11249*

❹ GRAND FERRY PARK

Distinct from the bustle and industrial character of Domino Park, Grand Ferry Park is a small and beautifully wooded enclave tucked behind the warehouse and factory buildings where Grand Street meets the East River. Shaded by thoughtfully planted dogwoods and evergreens, benches look out at the bridge and the East Village across the water. Grand Ferry Park is a popular spot for watching the sunset behind the city. A red-brick chimney from a former Pfizer penicillin manufactory stands like a sculpture among the trees. **Grand Street at the East River, Brooklyn, NY 11249**

❺ ODDFELLOWS ICE CREAM PARLOR

Equal parts nostalgic and experimental, Oddfellows is a charming ice cream shop with a store that feels like a portal back to the 1950s. Decked out in stars, stripes, and ice cream parlor Americana, it's the kind of place where you want to sit at the counter for sundaes or to share a milkshake with two straws. The flavors on offer are always changing—sometimes the menu of specials changes a few times during a single day—and include fun takes on classic American ingredients, from Cookies and Milk to PB&J. **175 Kent Avenue, Brooklyn, NY 11249**

❻ EAST RIVER STATE PARK

East River State Park is the largest park on the Williamsburg waterfront and a perfect reflection of the neighborhood's culture. Sandwiched between shiny new apartment buildings to the south and shops and warehouse buildings that line the streets to the north and east, the park has spacious lawns, pathways between plantings of trees, benches and picnic tables, and a sandy beach along the river. The park is also home to one of the city's greatest culinary endeavors: Smorgasburg, the largest outdoor food market in the country, which occupies a large space at the southern end of the park on Saturdays from spring through fall, with more than two hundred vendors of everything from kimchi to fro-yo. *90 Kent Avenue, Brooklyn, NY 11211*

❼ ARTISTS & FLEAS WILLIAMS-BURG

Housed inside a light and spacious former warehouse just a block away from the waterfront, the Williamsburg Artists & Fleas is a paradise for shoppers and collectors of anything from quirky jewelry to vintage clothing, crafts, and design objects. The market is one of the neighborhood's liveliest scenes every weekend, with thousands of people passing through—picking up coffees at the bar on the way in—and more than seventy-five vendors, from independent young designers to outposts of more established stores like Eat Records and the Strand bookstore. *70 North 7th Street, Brooklyn, NY 11249*

⑧ KINFOLK

The headquarters of one of the brands that defines contemporary cool is also a cute store, bar, and café. Kinfolk has been around only for a decade, but its encapsulation of international street style—informed by its founders, who come from New York, Los Angeles, and Tokyo—has made it a defining influence on Brooklyn cool. Inside its airy, warm, and cleanly designed space at 90 Wythe, the store carries magazines, books, notecards, and other objects among the clothing, and you can sit with a coffee at the enormous window onto Wythe Avenue, which rolls up to open the café to the fresh air in warmer months. *90 Wythe Avenue, Brooklyn, NY 11249*

⑨ WYTHE HOTEL

The Wythe is one of the coolest hotels in Brooklyn and a hugely popular venue for eating and drinking in its own right. Set inside a beautiful former barrel factory building, its biggest draw is the Ides rooftop bar, a huge space with Art Deco–inspired decor and unrivaled panoramic views, with the low lights of Brooklyn glittering on three sides below and the silhouette of the Manhattan skyline across the East River to the west. *80 Wythe Avenue, Brooklyn, NY 11249*

⑩ DU'S DONUTS

Hidden in a small plaza on the ground floor of the William Vale Hotel, Du's Donuts is a competitor—along with the Doughnut Plant and Peter Pan in

Greenpoint—for the title of the city's best doughnut. Named for its owner, Wylie Dufresne—a celebrated chef and, in his previous incarnation as head chef of major Manhattan restaurants, a pioneer in molecular gastronomy—Du's makes rich cake doughnuts with twists on familiar flavors, from blueberry crumble to brown butter key lime. *107 North 12th Street, Brooklyn, NY 11249*

⓫ CHEZ MA TANTE

A neighborhood favorite, Chez Ma Tante is a French Canadian bistro with a stylish but warm and welcoming vibe. Candlelit and romantic by night, with a dark wood bar in the middle of the dining room where you can sip cocktails and survey the restaurant in the giant mirrors, it's also a lively scene by day. The menu is a mix of French bistro classics, from steak to chicken liver paté, with British and American influences thrown in; their kedgeree is one of the few in the city, and their famously fluffy and ever-so-slightly burned pancakes are their calling card. *90 Calyer Street, Brooklyn, NY 11222*

⓬ WORD BOOKSTORE

Occupying a charming corner storefront, Word is a cozy neighborhood bookstore that regularly hosts literary events. Decidedly independent, it doesn't always stock the full list of mainstream bestsellers, but instead has a thoughtful selection of fiction and nonfiction books with a liberal and artistic leaning. The store is particularly beloved for the consistently interesting staff picks, which they put a lot of time and effort into and publish online as well as on special shelves in the store. *126 Franklin Avenue, Brooklyn, NY 11222*

⓭ HOMECOMING

An unusual marriage of garden store, interiors shop, bookstore, and café, Homecoming is the epitome of the warm but minimal Brooklyn aesthetic. They carry plants and flowers suited to the subdued light of a New York apartment, as well as lovely terra-cotta and porcelain pots to keep them in. Then there are vases, glasses, dinnerware, and other assorted objects for the kitchen and home. Scattered among the plants and objects are books and magazines, most on the subjects of architecture, food, gardens, and interiors. And almost hidden among the greenery is a coffee bar, so you can refuel with warm drinks and snacks as you browse. *107 Franklin Avenue, Brooklyn, NY 11222*

⓮ PAULIE GEE'S

Paulie Gee's is regarded by many as the very best pizza in the city. Though they opened a slice shop on Franklin Avenue in 2018, their original location on Greenpoint Avenue, which opened in 2010, famously serves full pies for in-house diners only—no slices, no takeout, no reservations, no delivery. The pies are made in a genuine Neapolitan wood-burning oven and are playful creations that range from the classic to the downright experimental—the Brisket 5-0 brings together BBQ and pineapple, and the Frankel is as close to a Reuben sandwich as pizza can get. There's always a line for a table, but it's worth the wait. *60 Greenpoint Avenue, Brooklyn, NY 11222*

⓯ THE BROOKLYN BARGE

Brooklyn's answer to Chelsea's Frying Pan, the Brooklyn Barge is a floating bar moored just off the Greenpoint shore. The barge itself has a small bar serving drinks and of course offers views up and down the river; and, back along the gangway to shore, there's a larger second bar and a kitchen serving bar food. With picnic tables and umbrellas, as well as drinks served in plastic cups with colorful straws, the barge has a kitschy seaside charm to it, which is a surreal surprise to discover in the East River. *79 West Street, Brooklyn, NY 11222*

⓰ WNYC TRANSMITTER PARK

Transmitter Park is arguably the best spot on the Brooklyn waterfront to enjoy the sunrise or the sunset. Named for the radio tower that once stood here, the park has unobstructed views of Manhattan stretching from the Williamsburg Bridge to the south all the way up to the Chrysler Building and the skyscrapers of Midtown to the north. There's also a long pier that juts out into the East River, from the end of which you feel like you're halfway to Manhattan. At dawn, pink light is reflected in windows and facades across the river, and at sundown, one of the most iconic silhouettes of the city's skyline is in view across the river. *Greenpoint Avenue at the East River, Brooklyn, NY 11222*

⑰ SWEETLEAF COFFEE

One of the prettiest coffee shops in the whole city, Sweetleaf also happens to make some of the best coffee around, too. Set inside a beautifully restored single-story old warehouse building, the store is half coffee shop and half roastery—so Sweetleaf can roast their own beans and make their own blends on site. The interior is industrial but cozy, with exposed bricks and beams, old-fashioned light bulbs, simple wood and steel furniture, and large windows and doors that open onto the street so tables can spill into the fresh air in the summer. There's even a window in the wall that divides the building, so you can see the roasters at work. *159 Freeman Street, Brooklyn, NY 11222*

⑱ POLKA DOT

In a densely Polish neighborhood, among a plethora of bakeries, grocery stores, and restaurants devoted to different aspects of the national cuisine, Polka Dot stands out for having some of the best Polish food in the most fun and welcoming environment. The café-cum-delicatessen has everything from sweet treats like pychotka, pastries, and cheesecake to classic savory dishes like pierogi, blintzes, gulasz, and—hard to find among eastern European cuisine—an extensive range of vegetarian and vegan dishes. The café has the feel of a bright, cozy country kitchen, and you can eat there at the small wooden tables or take things to go, ordering coffee and pastries through the charming to-go window facing Manhattan Avenue. *726 Manhattan Avenue, Brooklyn, NY 11222*

BROOKLYN

EAST RIVER

OLD FULTON

DOUGHTY S
VINE ST

MIDDAGH ST

CRANBERRY ST

ORANGE ST

PINEAPPLE ST

CLARK ST

PIERREPONT ST

MONTAGUE ST

REMSEN ST

FURMAN ST

COLUMBIA HEIGHTS

WILLOW ST

HICKS ST

HICKS ST

HENRY ST

CADMAN PLAZA W

CADMAN PL

CLINTON ST

PLYMOUTH

WATER ST

MAIN ST

1
2
3
4
5
6
7
8
9
10
11
12
13

RIVIERA

EAST RIVER

The oldest part of Brooklyn—the neighborhoods of Brooklyn Heights, Dumbo, and Vinegar Hill, which face downtown Manhattan across the East River—are without question the borough's most beautiful. It's also one of the loveliest parts of the whole city to explore on foot, with a wonderful route easily mapped out that takes you along the waterfront and lets you slip inland and experience these remarkable and distinct enclaves—from the grand old esplanade in Brooklyn Heights, along paths winding through the newly landscaped Brooklyn Bridge Park, to the riverside streets of Dumbo and Vinegar Hill. The historic district of Brooklyn Heights is arguably the most gorgeous neighborhood anywhere in the city, with street after street of uninterrupted brownstones and townhouses leading down to the promenade. Its neighbor, Dumbo—so-called because it lies "down under the Manhattan Bridge overpass"—has transformed a historic industrial and shipping area into New York's chicest yuppie enclave, where trendy start-ups and tech companies share red-brick warehouse buildings with design stores and food markets. And walking into Vinegar Hill is like walking through the looking glass into *a magical realm in New York's past: little known by tourists, often overlooked by locals, and barely touched by the energy and commerce that surrounds it, the neighborhood's impossibly quiet streets feel like a quaint little upstate town, with just a couple of stores, a historic mansion, and one wonderful restaurant among townhouses overgrown with ivy and wisteria.*

1 BROOKLYN BOROUGH HALL

More beautiful and statelier in appearance than its counterpart at the other side of the Brooklyn Bridge, Borough Hall is one of the city's finest government buildings and sets the tone for this oldest part of downtown Brooklyn. Built in 1848, the hall is a Greek Revival building, sharing the grandeur of landmarks in Manhattan's financial district such as Federal Hall and the National Bank. A majestic stone staircase descends from a pillared colonnade, which looks out across the tree-lined Cadman Plaza Park toward the bridge. While it is an active government office, Borough Hall is also a lovely place to sit and people-watch across the park— and every fall it plays host to the Brooklyn Book Festival, when stalls of booksellers and independent publishers line the plaza and spaces within the building are given over to readings and events. *209 Joralemon Street, Brooklyn, NY 11201*

❷ BROOKLYN HISTORICAL SOCIETY

Hidden in plain view among the elegant nineteenth-century buildings of Brooklyn Heights, the Historical Society is a wonderful museum—and one of the borough's great architectural secrets. Finished in 1881 in the Renaissance Revival style, the building is a deep terra-cotta red, and its exterior is adorned with busts of culturally significant figures as diverse as Michelangelo and Benjamin Franklin. Inside—in addition to housing a great collection of objects, artworks, and papers depicting Brooklyn's history—the Othmer Library is among the most beautiful rooms in all New York, with stained-glass windows casting soft light onto dark wooden bookshelves, carved columns, and a balcony above the reading room. *128 Pierrepont Street, Brooklyn, NY 11201*

❸ BROOKLYN HEIGHTS PROMENADE

The views from the Brooklyn Heights Promenade, also known as the Esplanade, are some of the very best in the city. Backed by rows of exemplary and picturesque brownstones and townhouse buildings, the promenade is a tree-lined walkway that runs along the edge of the borough, looking out over Brooklyn Bridge Park to the East River, New York Harbor, the Brooklyn and Manhattan Bridges, and the Manhattan skyline beyond. Beautiful at any time of day or night—with panoramic vistas by sunlight and a galaxy of glittering

lights in the dark—the views are particularly special at sunset, when the sky turns pink and the facades of downtown Manhattan glow with its reflection. Benches line the walkway, so you can pause and take in the view. ***Promenade, between Pierrepont Street and the Fruit Street Sitting Area, Brooklyn, NY 11201***

4 FRUIT STREETS: CRANBERRY, ORANGE & PINEAPPLE STREETS

Brooklyn Heights is one of the city's most desirable neighborhoods, with block after block of landmarked brownstones and a history of famous residents from Walt Whitman to Lena Dunham. At the northern end, the charmingly named Fruit Streets form an enclave of the most picturesque blocks in the neighborhood. Purportedly

named by the influential local Hicks family—for whom Hicks Street is named and who coincidentally were also fruit merchants—these enchanting streets contain a great variety of nineteenth-century architecture, from wood-fronted cottages to red-brick carriage houses and magnificent brownstones. *Cranberry, Orange, and Pineapple Streets between Columbia Heights and Henry Street, Brooklyn, NY 11201*

❺ THE MIDDAGH HOUSE

Dating from the end of the eighteenth century to the beginning of the nineteenth century, the Middagh House is one of New York's oldest homes and unusual in being one of the few wood-fronted townhouses among the pristine red-brick and brownstone rows of Brooklyn Heights. A private home, it's not open to the public—but offers an amazing sight on the corner of Middagh and Willow Streets that transports you to a different time. *24 Middagh Street, Brooklyn, NY 11201*

❻ TRUMAN CAPOTE'S HOUSE

Another of the neighborhood's oldest buildings, the townhouse at 70 Willow Street was built in 1839. Its basement apartment was Truman Capote's home from 1955 to 1965, during which time he immortalized the area in *Brooklyn Heights: A Personal Memoir*. The address has become iconic for its association with the writer; pausing outside the house, a beautiful building in itself, has become a rite of passage for dedicated fans, on par with visiting Oscar Wilde's memorial at Père Lachaise Cemetery in Paris. ***70 Willow Street, Brooklyn, NY 11201***

❼ SQUIBB PARK BRIDGE

One of the perks of the extensive recent redevelopment of Brooklyn Bridge Park is this walkway, which connects Brooklyn Heights Promenade to the park on the waterfront below. Primarily a functional addition—there is no other quick way to go to and from the park from Brooklyn Heights above—the bridge has the added bonus of feeling like an adventure trail, zig-zagging across the Brooklyn–Queens Expressway and affording views up and down the river along the way. ***Bridge, between Columbia Heights and Brooklyn Bridge Park, Brooklyn, NY 11201***

❽ THE GRANITE PROSPECT

Walk the Brooklyn Bridge Park Greenway to the Granite Prospect, an imposing viewpoint constructed right at the water's edge. Resembling an oversized concrete staircase, the prospect faces the piers of downtown Manhattan and is situated on a part of the park that juts out into the East River—so sitting here feels as if you're watching the city from out on the water. *Brooklyn Bridge Park, near the East River Ferry station, Brooklyn, NY 11201*

❾ BARGEMUSIC

A treasure of the city's waterfront, Bargemusic is unique among the city's venues and one of the most magical places to experience music in the world. Founded more than forty years ago and set within a retired nineteenth-century barge that was active in New York Harbor for a century, Bargemusic is an intimate floating concert hall that plays host exclusively to chamber music. Bargemusic's artistic director, Mark Peskanov, is revered both as a violinist and as a champion of chamber music and American composers in particular. He draws on the success and influence of his career in classical music to bring an interesting program and phenomenal musicians to the venue year-round. Moored beneath the Brooklyn Bridge, the barge's wood-paneled performance room has windows looking out across the East River to downtown Manhattan, which means evening performances are illuminated by the flickering lights of the skyline. *Brooklyn Bridge Boulevard, Brooklyn, NY 11201*

❿ JANE'S CAROUSEL

Visible from the Brooklyn and Manhattan Bridges and a gem on the Brooklyn waterfront, Jane's Carousel was originally built in 1922 for a park in Ohio. After falling into disrepair, the carousel was purchased decades later and painstakingly restored for the redevelopment of the Empire Fulton Ferry State Park in Dumbo. Cleverly housed in a glass cube designed by the prize-winning architect Jean Nouvel, which allows it to operate year-round, the carousel was reopened at its current location in 2011 and has been a favorite ever since. No matter your age, it's difficult not to enjoy a spin around the carousel with views of the river, the bridges, and the city skyline all around you. *Old Dock Street, inside Empire Fulton Ferry State Park, Brooklyn, NY 11201*

⑪ ST. ANN'S WAREHOUSE

Beneath the Brooklyn Bridge, the Tobacco Warehouse has long been a defining feature of the Dumbo waterfront. Its distinctive red-brick walls stood empty for many years, and in recent years housed food vendors at the Smorgasburg fairs in the summertime. In 2018, St. Ann's Warehouse, a revered local contemporary theater and performance company, redeveloped the building into its permanent home, leaving the iconic walls intact and adding a beautiful glass-brick upper level as well as suitably theatrical lights and signs that illuminate the building by night. The space is now one of the cultural and architectural landmarks of the neighborhood with a terrific program of theater, dance, and music performances throughout the year. *45 Water Street, Brooklyn, NY 11201*

⑫ ONE GIRL COOKIES

The flagship location of an exceptional sweet-treat purveyor is a locals' favorite, not only for the baked goods and coffee offered inside but for the charming views of Dumbo's cobbled streets and the East River outside. You can rest inside with one of their famous (and famously large) whoopie pies or take something to go and follow the old steel train tracks embedded in the cobbles of Main Street to the park on the waterfront. *33 Main Street, Brooklyn, NY 11201*

⑬ WASHINGTON STREET AT WATER STREET

One of the great cinematic views in the whole of New York can be found on the corner of a Dumbo street. Looking west along Washington Street, particularly at the intersection of Water Street, you will find a strikingly graphic view of the blue-and-white tower of the Manhattan Bridge, framed by the red-brick walls of Washington Street's old warehouses. The view has been appreciated for more than a century, since the bridge went up in 1901, and was made famous by Sergio Leone in his epic New York film *Once Upon a Time in America*. **Washington Street at Water Street, Brooklyn, NY 11201**

⑭ DUMBO ARCHWAY

Manhattan Bridge was reserved as a storage facility for the city's Department of Transport. In 2007, the local community success-

fully lobbied for the space to be made public, and for more than a decade the archway has been one of the most popular and versatile spots in the neighborhood. From flea markets to yoga classes, food fairs to music performances, the space functions as a kind of urban park or public plaza and plays host to all manner of events and activities throughout the year. Rain or shine, in the shelter of the bridge, the archway is a great place to stop for a browse or a snack (perhaps from the Archway Cafe nearby) and appreciate the extraordinary architecture of the Dumbo streets. ***Water Street, under the Manhattan Bridge, Brooklyn, NY 11201***

⑮ MELVILLE HOUSE BOOKSTORE

It might take some exploring to find, but this quiet stretch of waterfront John Street—opposite an industrial-looking power facility—houses the office and bookstore of one of America's leading independent publishers. Melville House is most famous for publishing small and cleanly designed classics, and their store is a perfect reflection—intimate, and with a concise but smartly curated selection of books from Melville House and from other independent publishers. It's around the corner from a spacious outpost of Brooklyn Coffee Roasters, too. ***46 John Street, Brooklyn, NY 11201***

⑯ COMMANDANT'S HOUSE

At the far northern end of Dumbo in the small and secluded neighborhood of Vinegar Hill, a colonial-style mansion overlooks the Brooklyn Navy Yard. The Commandant's House—originally built for the Commandant of the Navy Yard, which until the mid-twentieth century was a thriving center for naval and maritime work—has been maintained as a private residence since 1964, when the navy yard closed. The house is hidden

behind iron gates and its grounds aren't open to the public, but it's a charming building to behold and an intriguing reminder of the neighborhood's past. These days, the navy yard is home to artists' and designers' studios, and Dumbo has become New York's "Silicone Alley," so little remains of the area's maritime history. **Evans Street, Brooklyn, NY 11201**

⑰ VINEGAR HILL HOUSE

One of the quietest and least-known neighborhoods in this part of town, Vinegar Hill feels like a glimpse of Brooklyn past, with untouched rows of Greek Revival townhouses overgrown with ivy, quaint corner storefronts, and vintage cars rusting quietly on silent streets. Hidden in the shadows of the Commandant's mansion, Vinegar Hill House is one of the few commercial spaces in the neighborhood—and a fantastic restaurant. The menu offers hearty, seasonal American cuisine, with rich meat and fish dishes and famously good wines and cocktails. With a fireplace in the cozy dining room and a beautiful garden in the back for outside dining in the warmer months, it's also one of Brooklyn's most romantic spots—and a perfect place to end a walk along the Riviera. **72 Hudson Street, Brooklyn, NY 11201**

BROWNSTONE

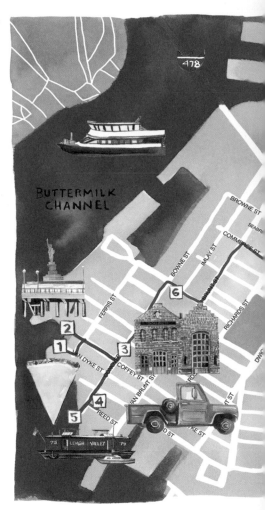

BROOKLYN

Further south down the waterfront from Brooklyn Heights, Red Hook is one of the few parts of New York that's not easily accessible by subway. Annexed from nearby areas by the Brooklyn–Queens Expressway—the elevated highway built in 1961, which was one of Robert Moses's many controversial contributions to New York's planning—Red Hook is also one of the quietest neighborhoods in the borough. With cobbled streets and century-old warehouses looking out over New York Harbor—and with lobster rolls, key lime pies, and a salty old-fashioned longshoremen's bar among its attractions—it has the feel of a seaside town and a unique atmosphere, which has inspired a young creative community to establish a budding arts and food scene. Most visitors, intimidated by the BQE or the walk from the subway, take a bus or car there; but a walk between Red Hook and the adjacent areas of Carroll Gardens and Gowanus is a lovely way to explore three beautiful and characterful neighborhoods.

Across the BQE, the unusually wide brownstone blocks of Carroll Gardens are home to a longstanding Italian American community, evidenced by bathtub shrines in front yards, Italian social clubs, and one of the finest places for pasta in the city. And the Gowanus Canal presents another kind of Brooklyn waterfront altogether: the canal, once spoiled by pollution from its surrounding industry, was designated a UNESCO superfund site in 2009 to clean its waters, and the peaceful streets around it now house a vibrant mix of historic architecture and contemporary buildings, with bars, restaurants, ice cream parlors, and even the city's only shuffleboard club among them.

❶ STEVE'S AUTHENTIC KEY LIME PIES

An unlikely Brooklyn institution and a cornerstone of the Red Hook community since it opened twenty years ago, Steve's Authentic Key Lime Pies has earned cult status by serving the best iteration in the city of that sweet, zesty southern dessert. Making every pie from scratch using only the freshest ingredients is what distinguishes Steve's from the competition. Set in suitably salty surroundings close to the docks at the end of Van Dyke Street, Steve's has picnic tables and benches outside for you to enjoy your pies on-site—but they're even nicer taken to go and eaten in Valentino Pier Park or elsewhere along the waterfront. *185 Van Dyke Street, Brooklyn, NY 11231*

❷ VALENTINO PIER PARK

In the seventeenth century, this point on the waterfront was an important dock for the new Dutch community taking shape in Brooklyn. Now, surrounded by a charming mix of new buildings and nineteenth-century warehouses, Valentino Pier Park affords some of the most idyllic views of green space anywhere in the borough. New walkways

jut out over the rocky shore, and piers extend into the waters known as the Buttermilk Channel, giving direct views of the Statue of Liberty and the rest of New York Harbor beyond. It's a perfect spot for a summer picnic with snacks from the stores nearby in Red Hook, a romantic date, a dog walk, or—if the locals are anything to go by—fishing off the quay. *Ferris Street between Coffey and Van Dyke Streets, Brooklyn, NY 11231*

❸ CACAO PRIETO

Hidden on a quiet cobbled street just a block from the water, Cacao Prieto is an unlikely but wonderful combination of chocolate factory and whiskey distillery. Set within a red-brick building designed to complement Red Hook's iconic nineteenth-century warehouses, the factory's refining machines share the beautiful space with distilling machines, which gives the shop inside—and in fact the whole block—an intoxicating mixture of rich and mouthwatering aromas. You can buy everything from exotic chocolate bars to cookies and cocoa powder in the store, or step next door into Widow Jane, the charming bar where you can sample cocktails made with the distillery's own spirits. Tours of the factory are fascinating—all the chocolate is made from sustainably sourced cacao in the Dominican Republic, and many of the machines are vintage—and it's impossible to resist a taste (or a drink) afterward. *218 Conover Street, Brooklyn, NY 11231*

❹ SUNNY'S BAR

Sunny's is a true throwback to a bygone time. Originally a watering hole for the fishermen and longshoremen that populated Red Hook in its industrial heyday, the bar changed over the decades as the neighborhood around it evolved—but it's retained a unique charm and eccentricity. For a period in the 1990s and 2000s, the bar operated as a kind of social club where locals would come to read stories and play music over drinks "given" to customers in exchange for "donations." With walls lined with paintings and curious artifacts (only some of which speak to the history of Red Hook), cozy booths, a long wooden bar, and a space for music and performances in the corner, Sunny's is warm and intimate and old-fashioned in the best way—and a drink there is a rite of passage for anyone visiting the neighborhood. *253 Conover Street, Brooklyn, NY 11231*

❺ WATERFRONT MUSEUM

Housed in a floating red railroad barge more than a century old, the Waterfront Barge Museum is something of an emblem of Red

Hook. Though modest in size, the museum houses a collection of objects that paint a vivid picture of the area's maritime history—and outside museum visiting hours, an educational space for the community, hosting classes, events, and other activities year-round. **290 Conover Street, Brooklyn, NY 11231**

❻ PIONEER WORKS

One of the cultural landmarks of Red Hook, Pioneer Works is a nonprofit venue for exhibitions, performances, and other arts and education programs that range from the local to the international. The stunning space—inside the beautifully renovated Pioneer Iron Works, the factory building that dates to the mid-nineteenth century and gave the street its name—is large enough to accommodate major installations as well as large-scale performances, so it has attracted an amazing range of supporters and exhibitors, from contemporary sculptors to cutting-edge choreographers and musicians. There are frequently great things to see here, and the building is worth exploring even aside from the artwork. Its Second Sundays series opens the space up every fortnight for people to see work and hear music from local artists, with food and drink on hand from Red Hook vendors. *159 Pioneer Street, Brooklyn, NY 11231*

❼ DEFONTE'S SANDWICH SHOP

Defonte's is the kind of place locals don't talk about in case the secret gets out. A classic Italian sandwich shop, Defonte's essentially does one thing incredibly well: old-school Italian American heros. The menu, on the boards behind the counter, is a list of favorites and new twists on the iconic sub—delicious soft rolls stuffed to bursting with fresh ingredients, from cured meats and cheeses to roasted peppers and eggplant. *379 Columbia Street, Brooklyn, NY 11231*

❽ THE AMAZING GARDEN AND SUMMIT STREET COMMUNITY GARDEN

Framing either end of a single block on Columbia Street, these two community gardens are welcome little oases of lush green space in an otherwise urban stretch between Red Hook and its next-door neighborhood, Carroll Gardens. Both were founded more than twenty years ago, in the 1990s, have been gardened and maintained by local green-thumbed residents since, and are open to the public. Both gardens host events organized by community members year-round, from summer cookouts to vegetable gardening workshops, but more than anything they are wonderful spots to take a break on a walk and pause among the flowers and trees. ***Columbia Street at Carroll and Summit Streets, Brooklyn, NY 11231***

➒ SACRED HEARTS CHURCH

Now more than 150 years old, the Sacred Hearts of Jesus and Mary and St. Stephen's Church is one of the most striking buildings in Carroll Gardens. Designed in the Gothic style, the church's unusually bright palette of red, white, and copper green makes it something of a beacon shining over the gray band of the Brooklyn–Queens Expressway, which divides Carroll Gardens from Red Hook. An important and beloved church in a historically Catholic Italian American community, the church is often busy, and is as beautiful on the inside as it is from the street, with cavernous vaulted ceilings and a gorgeous pipe organ presiding over the wood-paneled vestry. ***125 Summit Street, Brooklyn, NY 11231***

➓ COURT STREET GROCERS

In less than a decade, Court Street Grocers has grown from a single delicatessen to a beloved mini-chain with outposts around the city. Its Court Street location was the first and remains both a neighborhood favorite and an icon of the young but nostalgic Carroll Gardens culture (you'll see their tote bags everywhere you go, too). As well as serving award-winning classic sandwiches from the Reuben to the humble meatloaf, the store also sells delicious prepared dishes and relatively exotic treats from around the country—from condiments that break the Heinz and A-1 mold to candy bars that look like they were made in the 1950s. CSG even bottles their own drinks, which include their take on a pale ginger ale and a celery soda. Stop by to refuel or to pause with a coffee to people-watch on the bench outside. **485 Court Street, Brooklyn, NY 11231**

⑪ FRANKIES 457 SPUNTINO

Frankies is an authentically Italian American restaurant, with other outposts in Brooklyn and Manhattan and their own brand of olive oil in markets everywhere—but, more importantly, its original location has one of the most beautiful gardens of any restaurant in the city. Tucked away behind the restaurant, the garden is surrounded by

trees and has a Mediterranean feel to it, with olive trees and potted plants among the tables, clematis and honeysuckle climbing the walls, and strings of lights illuminating softly from above. Go for one of their perfect plates of pasta, like the cavatelli with sausage, and linger to make your wine last as long as you can. *457 Court Street, Brooklyn, NY 11231*

12 THE GREEN BUILDING

It's impossible to miss this curious old factory building alongside the Gowanus Canal—in part because of its striking green exterior and in part because you'll see a beautifully restored nineteenth-century horse's cart parked outside. Originally constructed to be a brass foundry in 1931, the building was transformed into its current incarnation as an events space in 2008 and for more than a decade has been one of Brooklyn's most prized venues. While the space is predominantly used for weddings and private parties, it's an attraction in its own right—and often the doors are left open between events, so you can wander in to see the gorgeous beamed ceilings and renovated interior, too. *452 Union Street, Brooklyn, NY 11231*

13 LAVENDER LAKE BAR

Legend has it that "Lavender Lake" was an ironic nickname coined in the nineteenth century for the notoriously dirty Gowanus Canal, which cuts through this part of Brooklyn and divides the neighborhoods of Carroll Gardens and Cobble Hill from Park Slope. These days, the canal is undergoing major cleaning, and the neighborhood of Gowanus—while not quite yet the Venice of Brooklyn—has become a desirable place to live, with quiet streets, not much commerce, and a mix of older industrial buildings and clean, new residential architecture. This popular bar sits right alongside the canal at the foot of the Carroll Street Bridge and has a spacious garden in the back, which makes it a lovely place for a drink. *383 Carroll Street, Brooklyn, NY 11231*

⓮ CARROLL STREET BRIDGE

The most picturesque bridge over the Gowanus Canal, the Carroll Street Bridge is one of just four retracting bridges left in the entire country (and one of two in New York City). Built in 1889 and designated a landmark nearly a century later in 1987, the bridge carries traffic over a lane of wooden planks, with pedestrians strolling narrow iron-fenced walkways on either side. Parts in the middle retract to either bank of the canal when boats need to pass by. Walk to the middle of the bridge and take in the views up and down the canal. *Carroll Street between Bond and Nevins Streets, Brooklyn, NY 11231*

⓯ ROYAL PALMS SHUFFLEBOARD CLUB

No longer only for the decks of cruise ships or Florida retirement communities, the fantastic game of shuffleboard now has a glorious home in a giant space alongside the canal in Gowanus. Opened in 2013 in an enormous factory building on Union Street, the Royal Palms is one of the neighborhood's greatest (and most unlikely) draws and a sight to behold even if you're not in the mood to play. Aquamarine shuffleboard courts line the space, and a cool playlist floats out over the sounds of "biscuits" sliding across the lacquered floor (one of the cofounders is a DJ). There's a beautifully lit bar and a bay for a rotating selection of food trucks, so you can drop by for a game or two or for drinks and a snack after a day exploring the neighborhood. *514 Union Street, Brooklyn, NY 11231*

INDEX